The Yachtsman's Pilot to the Western Isles

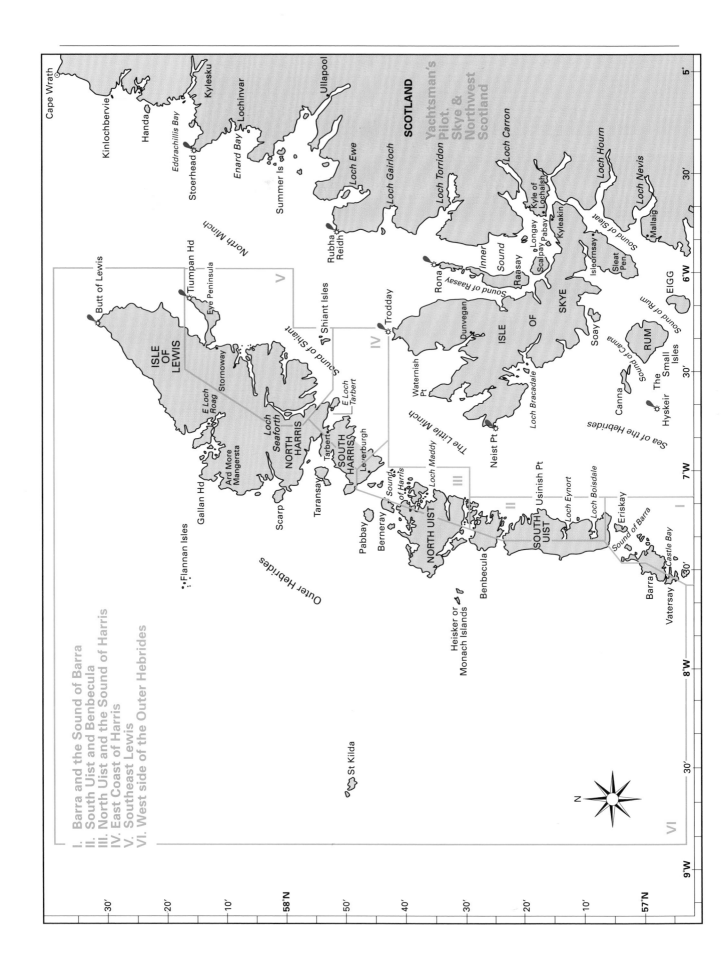

The Yachtsman's Pilot to the Western Isles

MARTIN LAWRENCE

Imray Laurie Norie & Wilson Ltd

Published by
Imray Laurie Norie & Wilson Ltd
Wych House St Ives
Cambridgeshire PE27 5BT England
☎ +44(0)1480 462114 *Fax* +44(0)1480 496109
Email ilnw@imray.com
www.imray.com
2003

© Martin Lawrence 2003
Martin Lawrence has asserted his right to be identified
as the author of this work in accordance with the
Copyright, Designs and Patents Act 1988.
1st edition 1996
2nd edition 2003

ISBN 0 85288 691 8

British Library Cataloguing in Publication Data.
A catalogue record for this book is available from the
British Library.

All photographs by the author unless otherwise credited.

PLANS
The plans in this guide are not to be used for navigation.
They are designed to support the text and should at all
times be used with navigational charts.
The plans and tidal information have been reproduced
with the permission of the Hydrographic Office of the
United Kingdom (Licence No. HO151/951101/01) and
the controller of Her Britannic Majesty's Stationery
Office.

CAUTION
Every effort has been made to ensure the accuracy of this
book. It contains selected information and thus is not
definitive and does not include all known information on
the subject in hand; this is particularly relevant to the
plans, which should not be used for navigation. The
author believes that its selection is a useful aid to
prudent navigation, but the safety of a vessel depends
ultimately on the judgement of the navigator, who
should assess all information, published or unpublished.

CORRECTIONS
The editors will be glad to receive any corrections,
information or suggestions which readers may consider
would improve the book, as new impressions will be
required from time to time. Letters should be addressed
to the Editor, *The Yachtsman's Pilot to the Western Isles*,
care of the publishers. The more precise the information
the better, but even partial or doubtful information is
helpful, if it is made clear what the doubts are.

CORRECTIONAL SUPPLEMENTS
This pilot book will be amended at intervals by the issue
of correctional supplements. These are published on the
internet at our web site www.imray.com and may be
downloaded free of charge. Printed copies are also
available on request from the publishers at the above
address.

The last input of technical information was October
2003.

Printed in Great Britain at The Bath Press, Scotland

Contents

Foreword

As an aquatic native living and working in Lochmaddy, it gives me great pleasure to welcome the most elaborate sailing directions ever published for the Outer Hebrides. The greater detail combined with sea-level, hilltop and aerial photographs extends the value of the book beyond that of visiting yachtsmen to include all of the island fishing and boating fraternity.

In 1963, Martin Lawrence and his wife Jean had their first Hebridean cruise in an Osprey dinghy, which they shipped across the Minch. Since then, Martin has put his architectural, observational and draughtsmanship skills to fine use in producing a whole series of sailing directions. Initially this was in updating and extending the famous Clyde Cruising Club 'Bible' and is now with the illustrated Imray series.

On a summer evening, it is lovely to see the sun sparkling on the sails of yachts as they scamper in to tie up on the visitors moorings. These moorings have been a great asset and enable whole crews to come ashore together and spend a day exploring the more beautiful Western Coasts off the Hebrides with the many beaches of pure white sand, or casting a line in some of the many lochs so full of native brown trout. Although most boats crowd on to the moorings, many still anchor either overnight or for part of a day in the secluded corners which abound in every Hebridean sea loch, and the book gives clear guidance for most of these.

On behalf of all islanders I welcome you to enhance your visit by coming ashore, stretching your legs, talking to local residents and joining them at any current event, rather than just spending the whole evening with other visitors in the local hotel even though it is so handy for your landing.

Dr John Macleod MBE
Lochmaddy
North Uist

Preface

The first pilot book specifically for yachts cruising on the west coast of Scotland was Volume 5 of Frank Cowper's *Sailing Tours,* written nearly 100 years ago. Cowper had no great enthusiasm for the Outer Hebrides: 'As regards a cruise among the Outer Hebrides . . . I do not think unless one has unlimited time the scenery is worth the trouble. Rocks, endless rocks; land barren, bleak, mountainous here and there, but with mountains of no great height . . . Of all the shelters none is better than Stornoway and everything worth seeing can be visited from there'. Certainly there is little 'worth seeing' in the way of monuments or artificial entertainments; if you need more than the sea and the hills, seabirds, seals and porpoises, plants and 'endless rocks' for entertainment, and the constant inconstancy of the weather, and solitude (which is perhaps more highly regarded now than in Cowper's time), you may be disappointed.

A meticulous survey of the Outer Hebrides was carried out between 1845 and 1860 under the command of Captain Henry Otter and Captain F W L Thomas, and the accuracy achieved with the methods available to them is almost incredible. A few areas such as the Sound of Harris have been resurveyed more recently but most current charts are derived from these old surveys.

The Outer Hebrides is a marginal area, not well enough known for every detail to have been precisely described, and referred to by one yachtsman as 'here-be-dragons country'.

An article by Michael Gilkes in the Royal Cruising Club *Journal* led me to the old Admiralty surveys at a time when I had undertaken to redraw the plans for Clyde Cruising Club's *Sailing Directions,* to correspond with the 'metrication' of Admiralty charts.

Since 1976 I have been gathering information from many sources previously unexamined, such as the surveys described above, and RAF survey photographs which have provided detail available from no other source. The initial product of these investigations was the Clyde Cruising Club's *Outer Hebrides Sailing Directions* of 1979, the first of a series of volumes to replace the classic *Sailing Directions West Coast of Scotland.* Others followed, and the *Outer Hebrides* was rewritten by the subsequent editor, Dempster Maclure.

An initiative by Nigel Gardner led in turn to this present series of yachtsmen's pilots, using the more comprehensive resources available to Imrays to include photos and plans with colour and shading. A volume entitled *Castle Bay to Cape Wrath* was published, but the material has grown so much that it has become appropriate to divide that volume in two. Incidentally, Imray's involvement on the West Coast is of long standing: a chart of the northwest of Scotland was published by Laurie and Whittle, a predecessor of Imray, Laurie, Norie and Wilson, in 1794 – about 50 years before the first Admiralty chart of the West Coast.

While I have sailed on the West Coast for more than 30 years, I make no claim to personal knowledge of every anchorage described, and my purpose is to gather information from every available source and present it in the clearest possible way. Many people know far more about individual areas than I do, and some of them have generously given me the benefit of their experience and taken a great deal of time to discuss their observations. However, the greatest single source of value which this book has must be the unpublished Admiralty surveys. In return I have only been able to supply a few observations to the Hydrographic Office, which have always been gratefully acknowledged.

I do urge any yachtsman who knows of uncharted hazards or features which would be of use to other mariners to supply the fullest details to the Hydrographic Office. The Office relies heavily on information from users, particularly for less-frequented areas, and is not sufficiently well funded to be able to update its surveys except for some very pressing commercial or military purpose.

It is the constant complaint of writers of pilot books, whether published commercially or by clubs, that they receive little support from users. However, a select band of individuals has regularly provided information to update the *Yachtsman's Pilots*, and others occasionally when they have come across points worth mentioning. I hope I have included them all in the acknowledgements below.

Photographs from sea level, from the air and from hilltops have been used to supplement the plans and descriptions. Ideally, photos should be taken at low spring tides to reveal as many hazards as possible, and I was fortunate to be able to fly over the Hebrides on a brilliantly clear day around a low spring tide combined with high pressure. It is not always possible to present all relevant information on facing pages, but plans and photos should also be looked for on pages preceding and following the text.

Acknowledgements
Valuable help was provided by the harbourmaster of Comhairle nan Eilean (Western Isles Council), Captain Calum Macleod (himself a small-boat sailor). Detailed information about new harbours was provided by Waterman Partners, civil engineers, and the engineer responsible for these works, Joe Magee. The staff of the Map Room of the National Library of Scotland have been patiently dealing with my requests for obscure information for many years.

I am particularly grateful to the following for various help with this volume: Robert Arnold, The Brathay Exploration Group of Cumbria, Nigel Gardner, David Leaver (MV *Guideliner*), Donald Angus Macaskill and Donald Maclean of Berneray, Donald John Maclennan of Cheesebay (North Uist), Dr John Macleod of Lochmaddy, Paul McNeill of Westbound Adventures Sailing School, Alastair Pratt of Uig (Lewis), Richard Scholes and the British Gas Sailing Association, which provides a report at the end of each season, John and Mabel Shepherd, Norman and Gillian Smith (MY *Barcadale*), John Stewart of Kallin, and Martin Taylor of Benbecula. Harriet Lawrence made some of the drawings of views (apart from those which have been reproduced direct from old charts); my wife Jean took some of the photos; and photos by others are acknowledged alongside each one.

Imray's editor meticulously checked every detail, and the final form of the plans may be attributed to Imray's cartographers, working from the outline drawings that I provided.

Many of the plans in this book are based on British Admiralty charts with the permission of the Hydrographer of the Navy and the sanction of HM Stationery Office, but above and beyond that I am extremely grateful to the Hydrographer and many of his staff who have taken time to search through archives and reply to requests for information.

There is much that is not fully known about parts of the Western Isles, and in spite of checking by many people it cannot be certain that errors have been eliminated. The fact that an anchorage or passage is described is no guarantee that it is usable by you on the day you are there. There could well be hazards which I have missed by luck rather than good management, and in spite of all the efforts of Imrays and others, there may be simple errors which have been overlooked – even the supplements to the *Admiralty Pilot* contain the occasional comment 'for E read W'. Scepticism and checking against all other information available is the safest course to adopt, with any directions. Before following the directions, plot the course on a large-scale chart and if you are confident that any errors will not be fatal, proceed; and if you disagree with what I have written, or find mistakes or changes, then please let me know, through the publishers.

The publishers are grateful to Elizabeth Cook who compiled the index.

Martin Lawrence
Mid Calder
2003

Key to Symbols used on plans

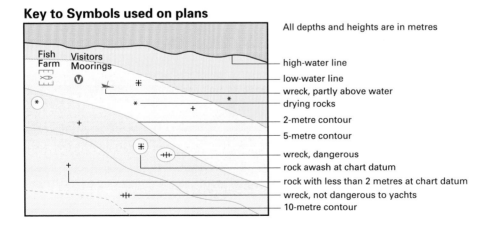

All depths and heights are in metres

- high-water line
- low-water line
- wreck, partly above water
- drying rocks
- 2-metre contour
- 5-metre contour
- wreck, dangerous
- rock awash at chart datum
- rock with less than 2 metres at chart datum
- wreck, not dangerous to yachts
- 10-metre contour

Fish Farm
Visitors Moorings

Introduction

The Western Isles, or Outer Hebrides, extend about 120 miles from Barra Head at the south-southwest to the Butt of Lewis at the north-northeast end, with a few distant outliers such as St Kilda and North Rona. There are many islands, many inlets, no marinas, almost no commercial harbours, few services and supplies, and fewer organised entertainments, but the natives are friendly. Daylight in summer is longer than in the English Channel owing to being 400-500 miles further north and the weather is, on the whole, less settled. But if you are prepared for the conditions at which this paragraph merely hints, you may experience some unique and memorable cruising. The whole area is increasingly at risk from fish farming and future oil development. Licences are being granted to drill for oil all round the coasts of the Western Isles.

This pilot sets out to provide, clearly and concisely, as much information as may be useful to small-boat visitors to the Western Isles. The upper limit of size for which it caters is a draught of 2 metres, and it includes information specifically applicable to shoal-draught boats – centreboarders, trailer-sailers, twin-keel boats and multihulls, and motor cruisers. In many anchorages there are parts which are only accessible to shoal-draught boats, particularly those which can dry out fairly upright. Some passages are only suitable for shoal-draught boats, and for the benefit of 'trailer-sailers' there is an appendix of launching and recovery places at the end of the book.

However, while the smallest boats, even cruising dinghies, may be at home in much of the area described in this pilot, they must be soundly equipped and competently handled by experienced crews. The Western Isles are no place for anyone who is unable to deal with adverse conditions which may arise unexpectedly. A good way to gain experience on the West Coast as a whole is to take a berth on one of the skippered charter yachts or instructional courses which are available.

At the closest, the islands lie 15 miles from Skye; the shortest crossing from the mainland south of Skye is about 45 miles, with anchorages at the Small Isles and on Skye to break the passage; from the mainland north of Skye the shortest crossing is 30 miles. Anyone who is capable of managing a yacht at a comparable distance from the shore whether in the North Sea, the Baltic, the English Channel, the Atlantic coast of France or the Irish Sea should have little problem on the west coast of Scotland.

Harbours and passages which are regularly used in the Western Isles are much better marked than elsewhere on the West Coast of Scotland, which will come as a relief to any skipper who has survived this far. However, there are still plenty of unmarked rocks, and strong tides in some passages. Conversely, commercial shipping is relatively scarce, and visibility is usually good – except in rain; fog, as such, is fairly rare.

To complete a round of generalisations, the climate is wetter and cooler than, for example, the south coast of England (although the further west you go, out of the lee of the hills, the drier the weather), but a compensating factor is the longer daylight in summer, so that you rarely need to sail at night.

Equipment should be as robust and reliable as for a yacht going a similar distance offshore anywhere in the English Channel or the North Sea, and a more comprehensive stock of spare parts carried, owing to the distance from sources of supply.

So many yachts are now kept in marinas and only sail to another marina, or to a harbour, that anchoring is no longer an everyday operation, but on the West Coast it is essential that the crew is thoroughly familiar with anchor handling. You should have at least two anchors, of the sizes recommended by anchor manufacturers or independent reference books rather than those supplied as standard by boat builders, which are often on the light side. Chain rather than rope will restrain a yacht from roving around in gusts, but if you do use rope it will help to have an 'angel', a weight which can be let down to the seabed on a traveller. Whatever the design of the anchor there is

Approaching Loch Bhrollum

1

no substitute for weight and I suspect that the reputation some anchorages have for poor holding may be due to many yachts having inadequate anchors. Attention should be devoted to ease of handling; unless you stick to places with visitors moorings (and there's no guarantee that one will be free) you will be using the anchor frequently.

Man-made features such as fish farms appear and disappear so frequently that it may only be possible to say that they were present or absent at a particular date, which may no longer be the case a few months later. Where a fish farm has existed, or was marked on a chart, but has been observed not to exist the fact may be noted; likewise an apparently uncharted obstruction may be noted. This depends entirely on some observer noting and reporting the fact and no responsibility can be accepted for the accuracy of such observations.

Chartering Charter boats are available, both for bareboat and skippered charters, reasonably near to the Western Isles, from Armadale and Badachro, as well as from further south. Many of the operators are members of the Association of Scottish Yacht Charterers, whose brochure can be obtained from The Secretary, ASYC, 7 Torinturk, by Tarbert, Argyll PA29 6YE UK ☎/*Fax* +44 (0) 1880 820012 www.asyc.co.uk *Email*: info@asyc.co.uk. Most operators also advertise in yachting magazines.

Charts This pilot is not intended as a substitute for Admiralty charts. Although many of the plans in the book are of a larger scale than the charts and include more detail, they only cover small areas, and it is essential to have a comprehensive set of charts at both small and large scales. A complete list of current charts and Ordnance Survey maps is given in Appendix II. Some important new editions have been published recently.

Certain obsolete charts show more detail than any current one and sometimes on a larger scale, but the soundings are in feet and fathoms. They should, of course, only be used to supplement current charts, not as a substitute for them; although it has been observed that 'rocks don't move', new hazards are discovered (sometimes the hard way), buoys are moved around, and new features are constructed.

For passage-making, Imray's charts C65, C66 and C67 at around 1:150,000 give better coverage than any current Admiralty charts and are more convenient to use.

The horizontal datum of Admiralty charts of home waters is in the process of being changed. The difference in the co-ordinates of a position may be as much as 100 metres, which is enough to miss the entrance of a harbour in poor visibility, or to fail to avoid concealed hazards, especially if the navigator is putting undue faith in the precision of electronic position fixing.

The newer charts are clearly marked WGS84, and production of editions of charts using this datum began to appear in 2000 (eg chart 2642 Sound of Harris).

On some GPS receivers the appropriate datum can be selected; that used by default is WGS84, but the older datum, OSGB36, may not always be identified on the chart. This is also the datum for Ordnance Survey maps.

If you have a chart with an unidentified datum and a GPS receiver on which the datum cannot be selected, allow at least 100 metres margin. Within the area of each chart, take an early opportunity to calibrate your GPS with a known charted object. Within the area covered by this Pilot the shift from the position given by GPS receivers calibrated to WGS84 to charts set out to OSGB36 varies between 0·0 and 0·01 minutes northward and between 0·06 and 0·08 minutes eastward.

Maps published by Ordnance Survey at 1:50,000 provide more topographical detail than current hydrographic charts . Where the charts are at a small scale the Ordnance Survey maps may also be some help for navigation. OS *Explorer* maps at 1:25,000 are occasionally useful where there is no Admiralty chart at a sufficiently large scale. An index sheet of all OS maps is available from larger bookshops and from Ordnance Survey, Romsey Road Southampton, SO16 4GU ☎ 08456 05050 *Fax* 023 8079 2615, as well as on the Internet at www.ordnancesurvey.co.uk

Travel

Transport There are good roads to those places on the mainland coast where one might make crew changes, although they are often narrow and patience needs to be exercised with touring coaches, caravans and heavy lorries.

Skye is now reached from the mainland by a bridge on which very heavy tolls are charged, and a car ferry to Skye runs from Mallaig to Armadale. Car ferries to the Outer Hebrides operate from Oban to Castlebay and Lochboisdale, and from Mallaig to Castlebay; from Uig on Skye to Lochmaddy and Tarbert (Harris), and from Ullapool to Stornoway.

Trains to Mallaig run from Glasgow via Fort William, and to Kyle of Lochalsh from Inverness. Air services to Barra, Benbecula and Stornoway operate from Glasgow and Inverness. A variety of long-distance and local bus services reach most places eventually.

Passage making

Except for crossing the Minch and on the west side of the islands, the distance between the entrances of sheltered anchorages is rarely more than 12 miles. Serious navigation is still necessary, but for much of the time it is a matter of pilotage by eye and satisfying yourself that what you see corresponds to the chart. The most useful position lines are transits

Ferry on Loch Maddy. Car ferries have little room to manoeuvre in the approach to the terminals

such as tangents of islands or beacons in line with headlands, and these should be picked out on the chart in advance. Compass bearings should of course also be taken, if only to avoid wrongly identifying a whole group of islands.

Some light beacons are inconspicuous structures and not mentioned as daymarks where they are not easily seen and identified.

At night Salient points and hazards in the Minches and in the approaches to lochs and inlets used by naval and commercial traffic are well enough lit, but in these latitudes there is little darkness in the summer months.

Visibility Usually good. Fog, as such, is rare. The *Admiralty Pilot* says that 'visibility of less than ½ mile may reach 3 days per month in midsummer' and visibility of less than 2 miles 'does not average more than 3 days per month during the worst summer weather at Stornoway and Tiree'.

Lobster and prawn creel floats Often encountered, even in the middle of the Minch and in the fairway of approaches to anchorages. Often floating lines lie upstream of the float, especially at low tide, and sometimes stray lines lie downstream.

Weather

Weather is extremely variable and any statistics can be interpreted so widely as to be of little help. After visibility, the aspects of most concern are wind speed and direction and rainfall. Rainfall is greatly affected by the proximity to high ground, and annual figures vary from less than 1000mm at the south end of the Outer Hebrides to between 1250 and 1800mm in the sea lochs on the east side of Harris.

Forecasting Schedules vary from year to year and a current almanac should be consulted. Apart from the shipping forecasts on BBC Radio 4, general (land) weather forecasts are often equally relevant where land and sea are so much intermingled.

Inshore Weather Forecasts are currently broadcast by Stornoway Coastguard at 0110, 0510, 0910, 1310, 1710, 2110 (UTC).

Tides

The spring range varies from 3·6 metres at Barra to 4·8 metres at Stornoway. Tidal streams are strong wherever the movement of a large body of water is constricted by narrows, and there are often overfalls at the seaward end of narrow passages, particularly with wind against tide. Overfalls also occur off many headlands, and eddies are formed, usually down-

'Are you sure. . .?' Grey Horse Channel, Sound of Harris

tide of a promontory or islet or even a submerged reef, but sometimes in a bay up-tide of the obstruction. There are also usually overfalls wherever two tidal streams meet.

Anchorages

The following very general observations may be helpful.

Steep high ground to windward is unlikely to provide good shelter – in fresh winds there may be turbulent gusts on its lee side, or the wind may be deflected to blow from a completely different direction, or funnel down a valley. Conversely, after a hot windless day there may be a strong katabatic wind down the slope, usually in the early morning – such conditions are by no means unknown in Scotland.

Within some anchorages there are often several suitable berths depending on conditions and it may not be practicable to describe them all, nor to mark each one on the plans. In any case, an anchorage suitable for a shoal-draught boat 6 metres long may be inaccessible to a 15-metre yacht with a draught of 2 metres, and a berth which would give shelter for the larger yacht might be uncomfortably exposed for the smaller.

Rivers, burns and streams generally carry down debris, often leaving a shallow or drying bank of stones, sand or silt, over which the unwary may swing – frequently in the middle of the night. The heads of lochs and inlets commonly dry off for more than ½ mile.

Within any anchorage the quality of the bottom may vary greatly. Mud is common (usually where there is little current), but its density may not be consistent and there are likely to be patches of rock, boulders and stones; also clay which tends to break out suddenly. Sand is also common, but sometimes it is so hard that an anchor, particularly a light one, will not dig in. Weed of all kinds appears to be on the increase, but this does vary from year to year.

Increasingly, moorings for yachts and fishing and other workboats, as well as fish farms, are being laid within established anchorages, preventing or restricting their use. Preservation of anchorages is one of the main functions of West Highlands Anchorage and Mooring Association (WHAM) who would like to hear about any apparently unauthorised obstruction; the honorary secretary of WHAM is Colin Davidson, Tigh an Eilean, Ardfern, Argyll PA34.

Fish farms are usually outwith the most popular places, but attempts are sometimes made to establish them in recognised anchorages as well. There are two main forms: cages for 'fin fish' (usually salmon), and rows of buoys from which ropes are suspended, on which shellfish are 'grown'. These buoys may have ropes between them, on or close to the surface. Fish cages may be moved around within a bay or inlet, often because they have created so much pollution that the fish can no longer live in the original location, so that they may not be found where shown on a chart or plan. The boundary of an area licensed for fish farming is sometimes marked by buoys, usually yellow and sometimes lit. These are often a long way from the cages, and there may or may not be moorings or other obstructions within the area marked out by the buoys.

Beacons are often not at the extreme end of the hazard which they mark.

Car ferries These run to very tight schedules and the space to manoeuvre at a ferry terminal is often restricted. Yachts must leave clear turning space near ferry terminals; apart from the safety aspect they may be disturbed by the wash from a ferry's bow thruster. Ferry schedules differ from day to day, especially those to Castle Bay, Lochboisdale, Lochmaddy, and Tarbert (Harris). It is very desirable to have a copy of Caledonian MacBrayne's current timetable (easily obtained from tourist offices and ferry offices or by post from Caledonian MacBrayne Ltd, The Ferry Terminal, Gourock PA19 1QP) to avoid conflict in the space around terminals.

Moorings Moorings for fishing boats are laid in many anchorages, but they may not be used in summer as their owners are often working on the Atlantic coast of the islands, and you may be invited to use a fisherman's mooring. Do not pick up a buoy unless you are sure that it is a mooring buoy and not marking creels for storing live prawns – or another yacht's anchor buoy!

Visitors moorings are arranged (as they have to be) to suit the largest boats likely to use them, and a boat on a mooring behaves differently from a boat at anchor. The effect is often to reduce the number of visiting boats which can use an anchorage. There is no guarantee that the mooring is suitable for any boat intending to use it.

The formerly recommended practice of rafting up two or more yachts on a single mooring is not now encouraged.

Welcome Ashore, an excellent booklet which details facilities provided for visitors by HIE, local authorities, hotels boatyards, marinas and other suppliers, is published intermittently by Sail Scotland, The Promenade, Largs KA30 8BQ. ☎ 01475 689899 *email* info@sailscotland.co.uk www.sailscotland.co.uk

Note that not all visitors moorings were regularly maintained in the past or covered by Public Liability Insurance. Future editions of *Welcome Ashore* will only include those which are covered by PLI.

Visitors moorings are provided and maintained by Western Isles Council. These are substantial blue plastic buoys, equipped with pick-up ropes.

Quays, piers, jetties, slips, linkspans These, and related structures, need some definition, as the categories overlap and a structure identified on the chart may have fallen into disuse, or been replaced by one of a different type, or have a description well above its status. The definitions used in this book are as follows, and give some indication of what you may expect to find.

A quay, wharf or pier is used by fishing boats and occasional coasters, and usually has at least 2 metres of water at its head at chart datum. It is often constructed of piles or open framing, or stone or concrete with vertical timber fendering, alongside which it is difficult for a small yacht to lie without a robust fender board. A pier projects from the shore, but a quay or wharf is either part of a harbour or parallel to the shore.

Ferry terminals serving the Outer Hebrides all have a linkspan for a bow-loading car ferry. The inner end is hinged and the outer end, supported between concrete towers, is raised or lowered to match the height of the ramp on the ferry, according to the state of the tide. The linkspan is usually at one end of a quay alongside which the ferry lies.

A jetty is smaller and, for yachts, more user-friendly but often dries alongside. Newer jetties are constructed of more or less smooth concrete, older ones of stone, often with a very uneven surface; a few are of timber.

A slip, or slipway, runs down at an angle into the water, although its outer end may be above water at low tide and it may be used by a ferry to an inshore island. There is sometimes sufficient depth for a yacht to go alongside a slip for a brief visit ashore for stores.

With the enormous growth in inshore fishing and fish-farming, many of these structures are in regular use by fishermen whose livelihood depends on being able to land their produce quickly, and yachts should take care not to obstruct them.

Dues are charged at some piers and harbours, even for a brief visit to take on water. The Western Isles Islands Council offers a 'season ticket' for a yacht to use two or several of its piers or harbours over a period of time.

Facilities

Considerable time, resourcefulness and imagination needs to be devoted to obtaining supplies or services but local people are in the same boat, as it were, and usually go out of their way to be helpful. Ferrymen, piermasters, hotel keepers, post-mistresses and fishermen are all useful and usually willing sources of information, and there are many services and sources of supply that are too irregular, ephemeral or unknown to be listed here. As an example of this, we were ashore on the east side of Harris one day, and one of the crew spotted an old yellow van, formerly a telephone engineer's, delivering milk; however, it would be unwise to report that milk was regularly available there.

There are no yachting services as such. Showers or baths are often available at hotels.

Diesel Available by hose at some small fishing harbours and quays, but do not expect quick service; fuel is supplied to yachts as a favour, although usually very willingly, but the person dispensing it may have better things to do than turn out to supply a relatively small quantity.

Water supplies Fairly rare at the quayside, and a yacht with built-in tanks should have a portable container or two, together with a straight-sided funnel, with which to fill the tank. A 20-metre hose of the flat variety on a reel, with a universal coupling to fit on any sort of tap, is also well worth carrying, as several small jetties have taps but no hoses. These small jetties, although they may only be approachable above half tide, are usually more convenient than the massive piled ferry piers, where the only hose may be too large to serve a yacht.

Eating ashore A few eating places, at which you may eat well, if mostly unadventurously, whether in a restaurant or a bar, are scattered throughout the islands. No recommendations are made as establishments may change hands – and standards – rapidly.

Fishing

Every boat should carry a rod and wet flies for brown trout. Each district has an estate office or angling club from which you can obtain a day permit. Many isolated anchorages have small lochs with fish in them. There's no point in going for salmon or sea trout on a sailing holiday.

Communications

Phone boxes Fairly well distributed and referred to where known, but the 'rationalisation' of the telephone service may lead to a reduction in their numbers.

Post offices Many now have very restricted hours of opening, and some which are mentioned may have been closed temporarily or permanently, although the information has been supplied by Post Office Counters.

The mountainous nature of this coast puts some areas out of range of either the coastguard or mobile phones.

Emergencies

Serious and immediate emergencies (including medical emergencies) are usually best referred to the coastguard. If you don't have VHF R/T but are able to get ashore (for example, if a crew member is ill), phone the coastguard or police. In less urgent cases, if attending a doctor's surgery do please attend at the advertised consulting times.

For less serious problems, such as a mechanical breakdown out of range of a boatyard, mechanics experienced at least with tractor or fishing-boat engines will often be found locally.

Coastguard The Maritime Rescue Subcentre for the area is at Stornoway ☎ 01851 702013.

Lifeboats Stationed within, or near, the limits of this volume at Castlebay, and Stornoway. The nearest on the mainland and Skye are at Mallaig, Loch Inver and Portree.

Notes on plans and pilotage directions

Generally the conventions used on Admiralty charts have been followed so that this pilot may be used in conjunction with them. See also *Charts* on page 2.

In each chapter information about charts, tides, dangers and marks relevant to the whole chapter comes first; then any passage directions, sometimes including certain anchorages where it is necessary to relate these to plans associated with the passages; then any branches from the main passage; and finally individual anchorages, usually in the same sequence as the passages described. Conspicuous features are listed to aid identification in poor visibility.

Lights, and any directions for making a passage or approach by night, are listed separately from the description of dangers and marks; as most of us sail mainly by day, this reduces the amount of information to be absorbed.

Bearings are from seaward and refer to true north. A few of the plans are not orientated with north at the top, in order to make the best use of the space available, but reference to the north point on the plan will make this clear.

Distances are given in nautical miles and cables (tenths of a nautical mile); a distance of less than ¼ cable is generally expressed in metres.

Co-ordinates to locate anchorages are approximate – waypoints for the entrance to an anchorage are specifically marked 'Waypoint'.

Depths and heights are given in metres to correspond with current Admiralty charts. Depths are related to current chart datum, which is generally lower than that on older charts. It is the lowest level to which the surface of the sea is expected to fall owing to astronomical causes. However, if high barometric pressure and/or strong offshore winds coincide with a low spring tide the water may fall below this level, in which case there will be less depth than shown on the chart or sketch plan.

Tides Heights of tides are represented by five sets of figures; these are: Mean High Water Springs (MHWS), Mean High Water Neaps (MHWN), Mean Tide Level (MTL), Mean Low Water Neaps (MLWN), Mean Low Water Springs (MLWS). The word 'Mean' is important because (for example) Low Water Springs in any particular fortnight may be substantially higher or lower than the mean. If you have tide tables which give heights of tides at Ullapool you will be able to relate the tide on any particular day to the equivalent figures there (5·2 3·9 3·0 2·1 0·7) and judge whether the rise and fall will be greater or less than the mean.

The difference between times of tides at Ullapool and at Dover may vary by as much as 40 minutes, so that tide tables for Ullapool will give more accurate results than those for Dover. Tide tables for Ullapool are included in all almanacs but are not published separately; but the constant for that port is +0110 relative to Oban, for which a booklet of tables is widely available.

Shelter The heading 'Shelter' at the beginning of each chapter implies an anchorage for which to run in reasonable visibility if the wind is increasing – ie before a gale has developed. It does not mean that it can be entered in any weather.

Place names are a frequent source of confusion and there are often differences between the name used on a current chart, on an older chart, by local people, and by yachtsmen. Anglicisations or translations are sometimes used quite arbitrarily on current charts among a nest of Gaelic names. The name on the current chart (or in the absence of a name on the chart, the OS map) is always given in this pilot, together with a popular name if the chart name is unpronounceable. Since the publication of *Castle Bay to Cape Wrath* the official spelling of some place names has been changed.

As place names often need to be spoken, the following approximate pronunciations of common words in names may be helpful:

Bagh	Bay
Bogha	Bo'
Caol	Kyle
Caolas	Kyles
Dubh	Doo
Mhor	Vore
Rubha	Ru'

Names of lochs and so on, are normally written as two words (Loch Boisdale, for example), but the name of a settlement beside the loch as a single word (Lochboisdale).

Aerial and hilltop photos often show more detail than can be included in the plans. All the aerial photos here were taken on a single day at a low spring tide with high pressure and brilliant visibility.

Photographs and views from sea level are used to illustrate transits and clearing marks, or to help identify landmarks, while transits are in some cases more clearly illustrated when the marks used are not actually aligned; where this is the case, the marks are indicated by pointers.

Changes, corrections, and supplements

While this book was being prepared for the press, major changes to navigational aids were afoot. There are also unresolved doubts about a few features, such as the drying height of certain rocks, particularly in remote or rarely visited areas. New editions of Admiralty charts are being prepared, which were not available at the time of writing. Further changes, such as super-quarries, fish farms and oil-related installations, may occur.

Readers are asked to bear this in mind, to make sure that they have the latest supplements (usually issued around May each year), and also to report any discrepancies, or even uncertainties, which may be further investigated by other readers.

This is greatly appreciated not only by the author and publishers, but also by the Hydrographic Office to whom any relevant information is forwarded.

I. Barra and the Sound of Barra

Crossing the Sea of the Hebrides to Barra and the Uists

Charts
1795, 1796 (1:100,000).

Tides
Tidal streams in the Sea of the Hebrides are generally weak except around Hyskeir
The north-going stream begins +0550 Ullapool (+0130 Dover)
The south-going stream begins –0010 Ullapool (–0430 Dover)
Around Humla the spring rate is 2½ knots with overfalls over all the rocks around Hyskeir. The sea breaks heavily up to 15 miles southwest of Hyskeir particularly in heavy weather and when wind and tide are opposed.

Dangers and marks

Cairns of Coll, above water and drying, extend 1½ miles north of Coll. A white tower, 8 metres in height, stands on Suil Gorm an islet ½ mile north of Coll, but a reef which dries 4 metres lies ½ mile further NNE.

Hyskeir (Oigh Sgeir), a rocky islet 5 miles southwest of Canna with a white lighthouse 39 metres in height.

Mill Rocks, awash and submerged, lie up to 2¼ miles southwest of Hyskeir; the north point of Eigg open south of Rum bearing 085° leads 1½ miles south of Mill Rocks.

Humla, a rock 5 metres high, 2 miles SSW of the west end of Canna, with rocks close west of it as well as between Humla and Canna, is marked by a green conical light buoy on its west side.

The bottom of the Sea of the Hebrides is very uneven and steep seas may be encountered throughout the area. The *Admiralty Pilot* states that the Sea of the Hebrides, between Tiree and Barra 'is about twice as rough in a given wind as the Minch'.

Directions

From Gunna Sound the passage is as from the Sound of Mull, without the hazard of the Cairns of Coll, but heavy overfalls may be encountered at the windward end of Gunna Sound.

Returning by this route, Gunna Sound is difficult to locate, but a radio mast on Ben Hough, 8 miles WSW of the Sound makes a good landmark.

From Sound of Mull to Castle Bay, Cairns of Coll must be watched for and the passage lies across

Hawes Bank which rises to 18 metres from more than 100 metres. Barra is identified by Heaval, which is 382 metres high. In poor visibility the 30-metre contour is absolutely as close as it is safe to approach Barra without being certain of your position.

From Sound of Mull to Loch Boisdale, in good visibility three groups of three hills are visible on South Uist. From south to north these are: south of Loch Boisdale, the Boisdale Hills between Loch Boisdale and Loch Eynort, and the more massive Beinn Mhor range at the north end of South Uist.

From Sound of Mull to Loch Maddy pass north of Hyskeir to avoid Mill Rocks. Eaval, south of Loch Eport, is noticeably wedge-shaped, and the prominent North Lee and South Lee, south of Loch Maddy help to identify the landfall.

Canna, about halfway across, has good shelter and access is easy. The passage east and north of Rum may be preferred for shelter and interest and is only about a mile longer. Note that submerged rocks extending further off the north end of Rum than previously charted were reported in 1992.

If passing between Muck and Eigg, note that drying rocks lie ¼ mile southwest of Eigg and that magnetic anomalies occur in that area.

For the passage along the southwest side of Skye and at Neist Point and for anchorages in the Small Isles including Canna see the *Yachtsman's Pilot to Skye and North West Scotland*.

Landmarks

Prominent landmarks when returning are: Small Isles (especially Rum), Hyskeir lighthouse, Ardnamurchan lighthouse, Cairns of Coll light beacon.

Lights (relevant to passage only)
Ardnamurchan LtHo Fl(2)20s55m24M Horn(2)20s
Cairns of Coll Lt bn Fl.12s23m10M
Hyskeir (Oigh Sgeir) Fl(3)30s41m24M
Humla Lt buoy Fl.G.6s
Barra Head LtHo Fl.15s208m18M
Usinish LtHo Fl.WR.20s54m19/15M

At night the approaches to Castle Bay, North Bay Barra, Eriskay, Loch Boisdale, Loch Carnan and Loch Maddy are well enough lit to be approached on a clear night.

Shelter

Shelter easily approached in reasonable visibility can be found at Canna, Vatersay Bay, Castle Bay, North

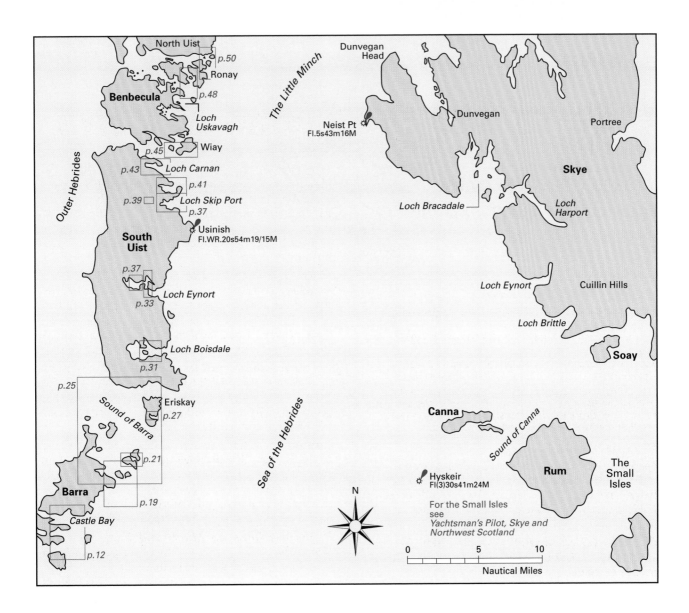

Bay, Eriskay, Loch Boisdale, Loch Skipport, Loch Eport (given sufficient power to stem a 3-knot tide), Loch Maddy.

Islands south of Barra

A chain of islands extends about 10 miles SSW of Castle Bay to Berneray. The southern islands of the Outer Hebrides have a maze of channels among them with a wide choice of anchorages and some spectacular sandy beaches.

Strong tides run through the sounds between them, with overfalls and eddies. Occasional anchorages may be found at some islands in quiet weather.

Chart 2769 (1:30,000); OS Explorer 452

Tides

In the passages between Mingulay, Pabbay, Sandray and Vatersay, tidal streams run at up to 4 knots

The east-going stream begins +0505 Ullapool (+0045 Dover)

The west-going stream begins –0140 Ullapool (–0600 Dover)

Constant –0110 Ullapool (–0530 Dover)

Height in metres

MHWS	MHWN	MTL	MLWN	MLWS
4·1	3·0	2·4	1·6	0·7

Passages between the islands south of Vatersay

In each of the sounds the tidal stream runs at between 2½ and 4 knots with turbulence at the down-tide end of the sounds and heavy overfalls with an opposing wind.

Sound of Berneray is only ¼ mile wide at its west end, and Shelter Rock which dries 2·4 metres lies a cable off the north side of Berneray.

BARRA

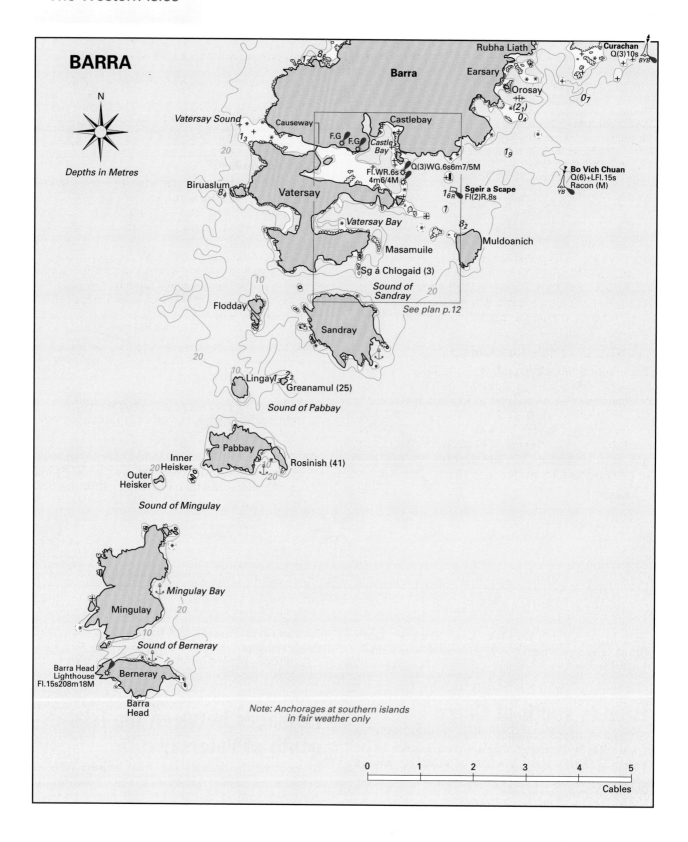

N

Depths in Metres

Barra

Rubha Liath

Curachan
Q(3)10s
BYB

Earsary

Vatersay Sound

Causeway

Castlebay

Orosay

F.G F.G
*Castle
Bay*

(2₁)

0₇

0₄

Biruaslum

Vatersay

Fl.WR.6s
4m6/4M

Q(3)WG.6s6m7/5M

1₉

Bo Vich Chuan
Q(6)+LFl.15s
Racon (M)
YB

8₄

1₆R

Sgeir a Scape
Fl(2)R.8s

Vatersay Bay

1

8₂

Muldoanich

Masamuile

Sg á Chlogaid (3)

*Sound of
Sandray*

20

See plan p.12

10

Flodday

Sandray

20

20

10

Lingay

2

Greanamul (25)

Sound of Pabbay

Pabbay

Inner
Heisker

20

Rosinish (41)

20

Outer
Heisker

20

Sound of Mingulay

Mingulay Bay

20

Mingulay

10

Sound of Berneray

Barra Head
Lighthouse
Fl.15s208m18M

Berneray

Barra
Head

*Note: Anchorages at southern islands
in fair weather only*

0   1   2   3   4   5

Cables

Tides

Tidal streams in the Sound of Berneray and close south of Berneray run at 2–2½ knots

The east-going stream begins –0600 Ullapool (+0205 Dover) and runs for 4¼ hours

The west-going stream begins –0145 Ullapool (–0605 Dover) and runs for 8¼ hours

At a point 3½ miles south of Berneray the east-going stream begins an hour earlier and and runs for 6½ hours, and the rate in each direction is 1½ knots

Constant –0105 Ullapool (–0525 Dover)

Height in metres

MHWS	MHWN	MTL	MLWN	MLWS
4·0	3·0	2·4	1·8	0·8

Anchorage

Berneray, (**Waypoint** at the east end of the Sound) 56°47'7N 7°37'0W. Occasional anchorage off the jetty and store house on the north side of the island east of Shelter Rock, which dries 2·4 metres, usually keeps the anchorage remarkably free from swell.

The Sounds of Mingulay and Pabbay

These sounds are clean and, at the west end of each, there are islets with a passage about mile wide between them. In the Sound of Pabbay, reefs which are partly above water lie 2 cables off the west side of Sandray and must be watched for if heading northwest by the east side of Flodday. A submerged spit at a depth of 2·2 metres extends 2 cables southwest from Vatersay.

Tides

The east-going stream begins +0505 Ullapool (+0045 Dover)

The west-going stream begins –0140 Ullapool (–0600 Dover)

In both sounds the east-going stream is the stronger, up to 3 knots at springs in Sound of Mingulay, and 4 knots in Sound of Pabbay with races and overfalls at the east ends of the sounds.

Sound of Sandray

This sound needs more care than the other sounds; it is partly blocked by a line of rocks which extend south from the east end of Vatersay to Sgeir a' Chlogaid, 3 metres high, in the middle of the east end of the sound.

A drying rock lies ¾ cable off the north side of Sandray south of Sgeir a' Chlogaid, and a 2-metre patch lies in the middle of the fairway.

At the west end of the Sound a rock which dries 1·1 metres lies in mid-channel.

Tides

In the Sound of Sandray tides turn at the same times and run at the same rate as in the Sound of Mingulay.

Lights

Barra HeadLtHo (Berneray) Fl.15s208m18M

At night There are no lights to assist a passage between the islands.

Anchorages

Mingulay, (**Waypoint** off the beach 56°48'7N 7°37'·0W), has occasional anchorage off the middle

Vatersay Bay, looking south towards Barra Head.

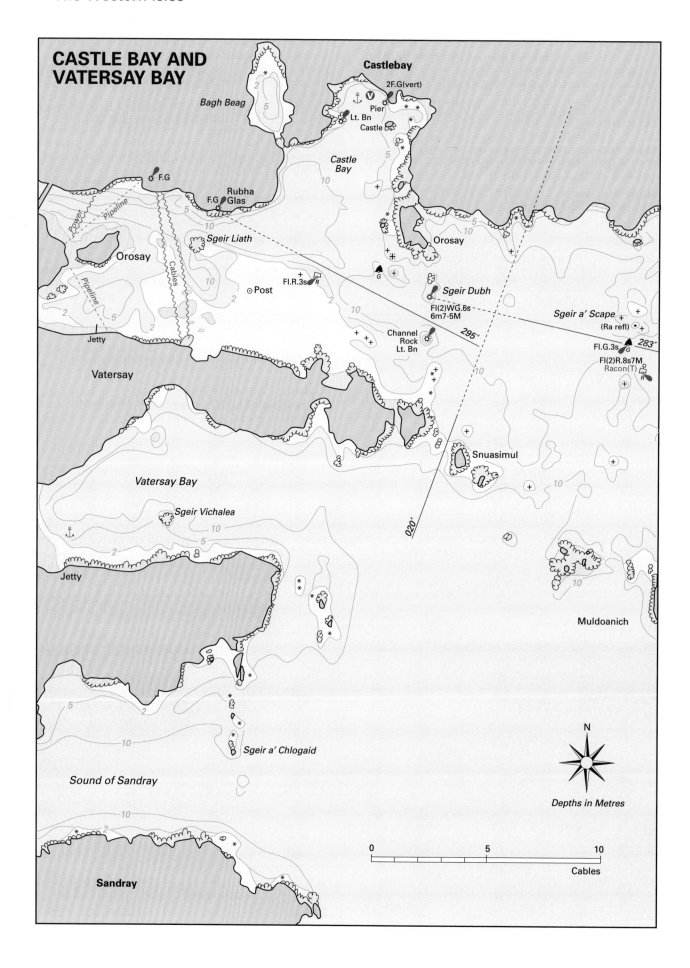

CASTLE BAY AND
VATERSAY BAY

Bagh Beag

Castlebay

2F.G(vert)

Pier

Lt. Bn
Castle

Castle
Bay

F.G

F.G Rubha
Glas

Sgeir Liath

Orosay

Orosay

Sgeir Dubh

Fl.R.3s R

Post

Channel
Rock
Lt. Bn

Fl(2)WG.6s
6m7-5M

Sgeir a' Scape
(Ra refl)

295°

283°

Fl.G.3s G

Fl(2)R.8s7M
Racon(T) R

Vatersay

Jetty

Vatersay Bay

Snuasimul

Sgeir Vichalea

Jetty

Muldoanich

N

Sgeir a' Chlogaid

Sound of Sandray

Depths in Metres

0   5   10

Cables

Sandray

of a sandy beach on the east side of the island, but in the most apparently calm weather there is often enough swell to capsize a dinghy; even if you can get ashore it may be difficult to launch a dinghy again. The best landing places are at either end of the beach. The west side of Mingulay is very impressive and it is worth sailing round the island in moderate weather.

Vatersay Bay, (**Waypoint** off S end of Muldoanich 56°54'N 7°26'·5W), on the east side of Vatersay, has a clean sandy beach at its head, partly sheltered by Muldoanich.

From the open sea the bay should be approached by the south side of Muldoanich as rocks are scattered northwest of that island. Sgeir Vichalea, a detached drying rock 2 cables from the south side of the bay, is unmarked. The best shelter is in the southwest corner of the bay, where there is a jetty, but this is uncomfortable in winds between northeast and southeast. The bottom is clean sand.

Passages

A fishermen's passage between Castle Bay and Vatersay Bay leads west of Snuasimul, a 17-metre islet east of the northeast point of Vatersay. Drying rocks extend more than 3 cables north from the east end of Uinessan, the islet west of Snuasimul, towards Sgeir Dubh light beacon.

A drying rock in the middle of the passage is avoided by keeping closer to a rock which stands above water on a drying reef northwest of Snuasimul.

Approaching from Castle Bay, leave *Channel Rock* light beacon to starboard and come round to approach the passage on a heading of 200°. Heading northwards through the passage steer 020° towards Beinn nan Carnan on Barra until on the leading line for the fairway to Castle Bay.

Sound of Vatersay and Castle Bay

Waypoint SE of Bo Vich Chuain buoy 56°56'N 7°23'W

Heaval, the main hill on Barra, together with Muldoanich, helps to identify the approach. The open bay provides less shelter than might be expected, and the holding is poor unless the anchor has been very well dug in, but moorings for visitors have been laid to the west of the pier. The west end of Sound of Vatersay is closed by a causeway.

Fishermen's passage from northwest; note rocks in foreground

Sound of Vatersay from SE. Fishermen's passage is just below the centre of the photo

Chart
2769 (1:30,000). OS map *31*; OS Explorer *452*

Tides
Streams are probably insignificant on account of the new causeway

Constant –0110 Ullapool (–0530 Dover)

Height in metres

MHWS	MHWN	MTL	MLWN	MLWS
4·3	3·0	2·4	1·6	0·5

Dangers and marks

Bo Vich Chuan, in a depth of 0·7 metre 1½ miles southeast of Barra, is marked by a south cardinal light buoy which serves as a landfall buoy (in poor visibility Curachan east cardinal, or Perch Rock south cardinal buoys in Sound of Barra might be mistaken for this if your navigation is adrift).

A pair of lateral light buoys about 2 miles west of Bo

Vatersay causeway from E

Vich Chuan marks rocks on either side of the fairway. Sgeir a' Scape, which dries, close north of the green light buoy, has the stump of a thin cylindrical beacon (or thick post) on it with a radar reflector.

Sgeir Dubh light beacon, 1 mile west of the red light buoy, is a conspicuous cylindrical tower with a platform at the top, near the south end of a drying reef.

Channel Rock light beacon marks drying rocks on the south side of the channel south of Sgeir Dubh. Submerged and drying rocks west of Orosay, northwest of Sgeir Dubh, are marked by a stbd-hand light buoy. Submerged and drying rocks lie up to 1½ cables offshore north of the buoy.

A new port-hand light buoy, 2 cables west of the stbd-hand light buoy above, marks the edge of shoals on the south side of Castle Bay.

The whole of the south side of the Sound of Vatersay is shoal, mostly sand with occasional submerged rocks. A perch, 2m in height, stands on Sgeir na Treanne which dries 2m ¼ mile SW of Sgeir Liath.

Leading beacons (white lattice towers 4 metres in height with orange triangular topmarks) stand on the south shore of Barra north of Sgeir Liath.

A light beacon stands on a drying reef on the west side of Castle Bay.

Fish cages lie off the west side of the bay south of Bagh Beag.

Directions

Pass south of Bo Vich Chuan light buoy, and steer to bring Sgeir Dubh light beacon in line with Sgeir Liath 283° and pass a cable north of the red light buoy. Pass between Sgeir Dubh and Channel Rock beacons; if making for moorings or anchorage off the village note the submerged rock lying west of a direct line between the buoy and the castle.

If making for the west end of the Sound of Vatersay or Cornaig Bay note the submerged rocks south of the leading line about ¼ mile ENE of Sgeir na Treanne perch.

For an inshore passage from North Bay and Sound of Barra see below.

Castle Bay, Barra from S

Lights

Bo Vich Chuan Q(6)+LFl.15s4M
Port-hand Lt buoy Fl(2)R.8s
Stbd-hand Lt buoy Fl.G.3s
Sgeir Dubh Q(3)WG.6s6m6/4M
Channel Rock Fl.WR.6s4m 6/4M
Stbd-hand Lt buoy Fl.G.3s
Port-hand Lt buoy Fl.R.3s
Ldg bns Rubha Glas 295° F.G.9m/15m11M
Reef W of Castle Fl.R.5s2m3M
Ferry terminal 2F.G(vert)3M

At night pass south of Bo Vich Chuan light buoy and steer with Sgeir Dubh light beacons in line 283°.

After passing north of the red light buoy, pass between Sgeir Dubh and Channel Rock beacons with the Rubha Glas leading lights in line bearing 295°.

Pass south of the stbd-hand light buoy and steer north to head between the reef light beacon and the ferry terminal.

If making for the west end of the Sound keep on the leading line to avoid shoals and submerged rocks south of the fairway.

Anchorages

The bay northeast of the castle is full of fishing-boat moorings and drying rocks. The pier beside the ferry terminal is often busy with fishing boats at night.

Moorings for visitors have been laid west of the ferry terminal. If no mooring is available, particular care must be taken to dig in the anchor, as the bottom is soft mud over hard sand.

Space must be left for ferries to manoeuvre at the terminal.

The area north of the reef on the west side of the bay is occupied by local fishing boats.

There is a good landing slip behind the linkspan.

Bagh Beag on the west side of Castle Bay has a narrow entrance with a sill which dries about 1·5 metres at its east side, on which stands a rock which dries 2·9 metres, slightly west of mid-channel.

Shellfish rafts are moored outside the entrance and numerous floats are moored inside and outside, as well as fish cages within, and a rock which dries 1·7 metres lies near the head of the inlet; apart from these obstructions there is nothing to prevent a yacht anchoring in Bagh Beag.

Cornaig Bay, south of the new causeway, has a pipeline lying across it. Drying rocks lie up to a cable off the northwest shore of the bay. A drying patch lies 1½ cables west of Sgeir Liath.

With sufficient rise of tide the bay may be approached by the south of Sgeir Liath, passing north of a post ¼ mile off the Vatersay shore which marks Sgeir na Treinne.

The bay on the east side of the causeway is a convenient anchorage, but there are many fishing boat moorings; a slipway is incorporated in the causeway, and yachts can go alongside after half flood (see photo).

Supplies

Diesel at Vatersay causeway and petrol at pumps in main street, water from hose at pier.

Shops (some hardware at Crofters' Co-op close west of ferry terminal; another hardware shop in the main street). Some shops are open in the evening when supplies arrive by a late ferry (which is the best time to buy fresh bread and milk). Post office, telephone, hotels. Showers and baths at Castlebay Hotel. Bank, doctor, tourist office, cycle hire. Water at slip at the Vatersay causeway, and phone nearby.

Piermaster's office beside CalMac ticket office (VHF).

Castle Bay, Barra

Coastal passage from Castle Bay to Sound of Barra

Charts

2769, 2770 (1:30,000)

Dangers and marks

Curachan (56°58'·3N 7°21'·3W), a rock 10 metres high 9 cables southeast of Bruernish, together with Red Rocks, a patch of submerged and awash rocks NNE of it, are marked by Curachan light buoy.

Passage notes

Many rocks lie inshore and the safe course is to pass southeast of Bo Vich Chuan and steer to pass east of Curachan and Curachan light buoy. Ben Scrien on Eriskay, open east of Gighay 015°, leads east of Curachan and surrounding dangers. However, a course further inshore as described below has been taken at a suitable rise of tide, in quiet weather and good visibility and with no swell. It would be as well to plot the passage on the chart before attempting it.

Passage between Curachan and Barra

From Castle Bay Pass south of Sgeir Dubh and a cable southeast of Rubha Charnain and Rubha Mor, keeping Sgeir Dubh beacon just in sight for the next ½ mile and then steer for Curachan until the reefs inshore of Curachan have been identified. Some of them appear to cover more than the figures on the chart indicate, so that a passage at the top of springs would be hazardous, although the clear passage between the reefs and Curachan is ½ mile wide.

From north to south Pass a cable west of Curachan and a cable southeast of Sgeir Fiaclach Beag; steer to pass a cable southeast of Rubha Mor with Am Meall at the southeast point of Vatersay just open of Rubha Mor, and when Sgeir Dubh comes open of Barra head towards it, keeping a cable offshore.

Breivig Bay (see photo and chart *2769*) is an occasional anchorage.

Lights

Curachan Lt buoy Q(3)10s
Eriskay Ldg Lts 285° both Oc.R.6s10m4M
Binch Rock Lt buoy Q(6)+LFl.15s

Breivig Bay, Barra, from SW

North Bay

Waypoint NE of Curachan lightbuoy 56°58'·7N 7°20'·3W

An alternative to Castle Bay, especially in southerly or westerly winds.

Tides

Constant –0110 Ullapool (–0530 Dover)

Height in metres

MHWS	MHWN	MTL	MLWN	MLWS
4·3	3·1	2·4	1·7	0·6

Dangers and marks

Curachan, Red Rocks, and Curachan light buoy are described above.

Beatson's Shoal, 4 cables south of Flodday, has a depth of 2·1 metres.

A fish-processing factory stands at Ardveenish, the north point of Bay Hirivagh.

Directions

From south Pass east and north of Curachan light buoy (alternatively pass 1 cable west of Curachan as described above) heading for the east side of Fuiay 356° until the factory is open of the southwest side of the channel.

From north Beatson's Shoal is a hazard if a heavy sea is running and the tide is low.

The approach to Ardveenish is marked by light buoys, as well as perches around the quay and slipway. No.1 port-hand buoy lies SW of Black Isles, and No.2 starboard-hand buoy west of Black Isles. Nos.3 and 4 are port-hand buoys further west.

A green perch with a white triangular topmark stands on the reef east of Ardveenish, and another at the slipway.

A white perch with a white topmark stands on a reef on the north side of a skerry south of the quay.

When Bay Hirivagh opens up, keep to the north side to avoid drying reefs off the south point and anchor as convenient in the north part of the bay.

Anchor SW of the quay, south of mooring buoys if there is enough depth, to keep clear of traffic to the jetty at the head of the bay.

Ardveenish Quay is accessible at all stages of tide; at the slipway there is 1 metre at the outer end at MLWS. Fishing boats unload catches in the late evening and it is unwise for yachts to be alongside at that time.

Supplies

Water and a public telephone are available at the quay; fuel and Calor Gas may be available from the fish-processing factory. Pub (meals and internet café), mobile shop, postbus to Castlebay, from jetty at head of the bay.

Northbay, Barra, from E

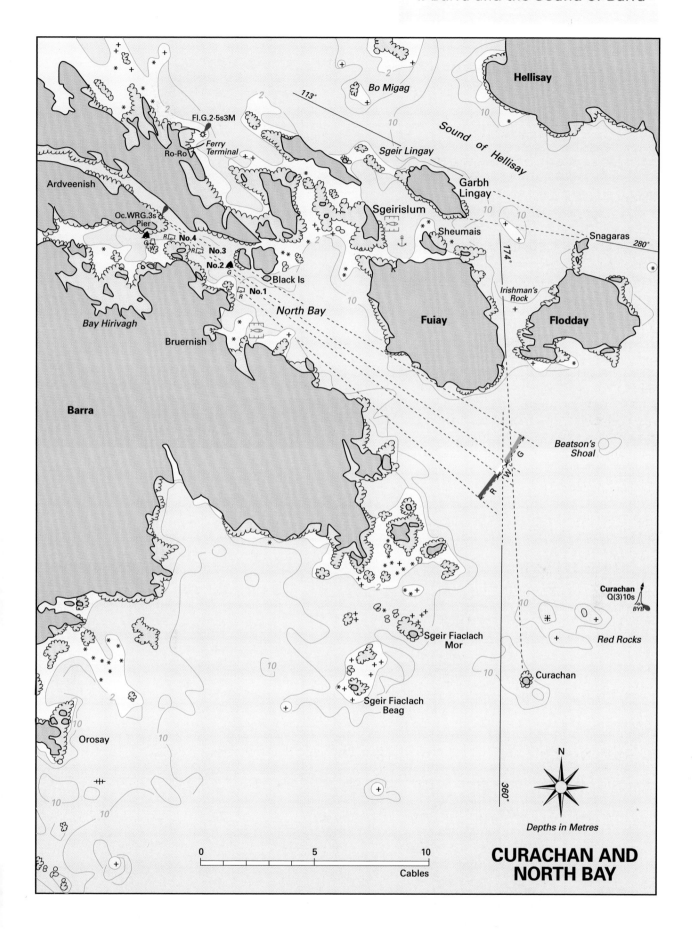

CURACHAN AND NORTH BAY

Depths in Metres

Northbay, Barra from W

Sgeirislum from E; Fuiay to left, Northbay to top centre left

Lights
Curachan Lt buoy Q(3)10s
Ardveenish Oc.WRG.3s 6m 9-6M
Ardveenish quay 2F.G(vert)
No.1 buoy Fl.R(2)8s
No.2 buoy Fl.G.2s
No.3 buoy Fl.R.2s
No.4 buoy Fl.R(3)5s

Sgeirislum

Waypoint at E end of Sound of Hellisay 57°00'·1N 7°20'W

North of Fuiay, Sgeirislum is enclosed by islands and partly occupied by fish cages.

Directions

From south Approach between Fuiay and Flodday, keeping to the west side of the passage at its north end to avoid Irishman's Rock which has a depth of 1·8 metres. A drying reef east of Eilean Sheumais is avoided by keeping Curachan open of the east shore of Fuiay 174°. Turn to port and pass close south of Garbh Lingay to avoid drying rocks north of the west end of Eilean Sheumais.

From east pass midway between Hellisay and Snagaras with the south side of Garbh Lingay open north of Snagaras 280° to pass north of a rock 1½ cables northeast of Flodday which dries 0·3 metre. Steer for the north side of Garbh Lingay until Curachan is in line with the east side of Fuiay to clear submerged rocks northwest of Flodday and pass south of Garbh Lingay as above.

From North Bay a narrow passage between reefs leads north of Black Isles and between Sgeirislum island and Fuiay, but this may not be usable at low water.

To pass through Sound of Hellisay to Oitir Mhor in the Sound of Barra keep Snagaras in line with the north side of Garbh Lingay 113° to avoid Bo Migag and Sgeir Lingay.

Hellisay and Gighay

Waypoint off SE entrance 57°00'·7N 7°19'·2W

A secluded sound between two islands both entrances of which are choked with rocks; part of the attraction is the challenge of finding the way in

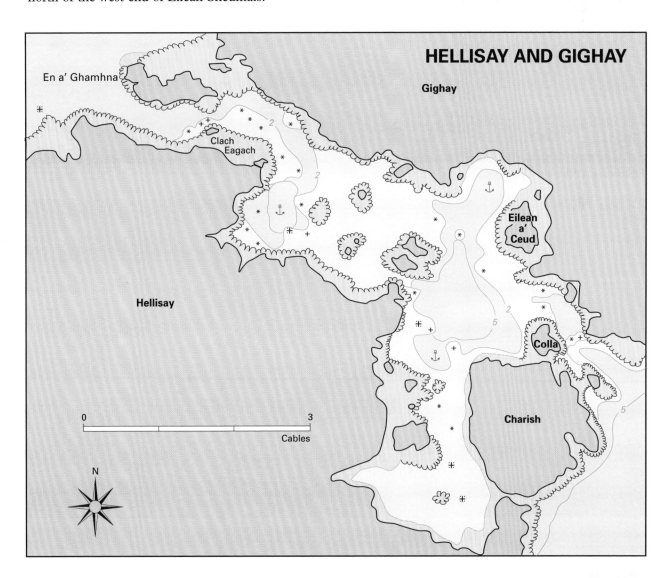

HELLISAY AND GIGHAY

Hellisay and Gighay from SE

Southeast entrance to Gighay anchorage from Gighay; note the
two drying rocks at the right

Gighay Sound, northwest entrance

without touching any of them. Once inside, each visiting yacht seems to find more rocks, or perhaps the same rocks in different positions, in spite of which a few boats find it worthwhile to go in.

Tides

There is some uncertainty about the direction of tidal streams in this sound. From most observations, it appears that the flood tide enters through both channels at 1½-2 knots at springs, although it has been stated to run right through from southeast to northwest, and may perhaps do so at neaps. The best time to approach is either at dead low water or about an hour before high water when the strength of the flood stream has eased but there is still some rise to lift a yacht off a rock if she should stick; it should be considered only if no sea is running. Do not assume that all existing rocks are shown on the plan.

Directions

The southeast entrance is relatively straight, but a rock in mid-channel east of Colla just dries with a submerged rock at a depth of 1 metre east of it. Another drying rock lies in mid-channel north of Colla with others on the north side of the channel.

A sandbank across the inner end is awash at chart datum. This entrance might best be used above half flood on a rising tide and only if there is no onshore sea. Two drying rocks ½ cable west and southwest of Eilean a' Ceud cover at about ¼ flood.

The northwest entrance winds between drying rocks and is best picked out at slack low water with a lookout at the bow. The clear passage shows pale over sand below water.

Steer initially for Clach Eagach, then northwest of it passing south of the reef which extends southeast from Eilean a' Ghamhna. Close the shore of Gighay to avoid rocks northeast of Clach Eagach before turning southeast to avoid a drying rock ½ cable west of a cairn (not easily seen) near the shore on Gighay.

Turn to head southwest, keeping ½ cable from the west side of the bay on Hellisay, to avoid drying rocks both inshore and further east. Anchorage can be found in this bay, but it should be examined carefully; if you find any more rocks do let me know.

Anchorages

The two most suitable anchorages at the east end are northwest of Eilean a' Ceud, and northwest of Charish. At the west end of the sound there should be swinging room in the southwest pool.

There is a relatively clear passage along the south shore south of the islets. A through passage on the north side is a matter of picking a way between rocks, although this is no worse than the northwest entrance itself.

The Sound of Barra

Waypoint S of Binch Rock buoy 57°01'·6N 7°17'W

The passage through the sound is tortuous although all the anchorages in this chapter can be approached from the east without using it. The chart has an elaborate sequence of courses for deeper-draught vessels which depend on the correct identification of a variety of natural features, but by keeping ¼ mile from Fuday yachts can avoid the rocks further east as described below. Overfalls occur northeast of Fuday with a southeast-going tide; that is, the in-going tide referred to below.

Light buoys marking the new ferry route across the Sound, as well as the old route (although the latter may be discontinued) are marked on the plan on page 25 as well as current editions of chart *2770*.

Tides

Tidal streams in the Sound of Barra run inward from both ends at once beginning +0530 Ullapool (+0110 Dover) and outward beginning −0045 Ullapool (−0505 Dover). They meet and separate in Oitir Mhor, east of Fuday, and west of Eriskay. Transits should be watched at all times to avoid being set off course.

Directions

From southeast approach between Stack Islands and Gighay heading for Fuday (if coming from Stack Islands do not head directly to pass north of Fuday). Pass ¼ mile northeast of Fuday until two prominent stone beacons on Fiaray are in line bearing 273°.

Keep on that line until Gighay has disappeared behind Fuday 135° astern and begin to come round to northwest – not too promptly, to avoid Drover Rocks – until the south side of Lingay is in line with the peak of Ben Scrien (on Eriskay) bearing 087°, see View D (the views are taken from a 19th-century chart).

If conditions are such that the overfalls northeast of Fuday might be troublesome, pass ¼ mile southwest of Stack Islands with the east side of Lingay touching the west side of Orosay 327·5° until Corran Ban shows north of Fuday 277° (View B). Steer on that bearing for ½ mile then northwest to pick up the beacons on Fiaray 273° as above.

Washington Reef, on which the sea usually breaks although its least depth is 3·7 metres, lies around 2 miles north of Fiaray.

Outer Hasgeir Fiaray, 2 miles NNE of Fiaray, dries 2·4 metres, but depending on the state of the sea a passage between Outer Hasgeir Fiaray and Washington Reef may be made by keeping the summit of Fuiay over the west side of Fuday 160° (see View A).

Weaver's Castle 290° leads eastward of Binch Rock

View D   Ben Scrien over south side of Lingay 87°

Lingay

View B   Corran Ban just open of Ru Hornish 277°

View A Fuiay over Dunan Ruadh

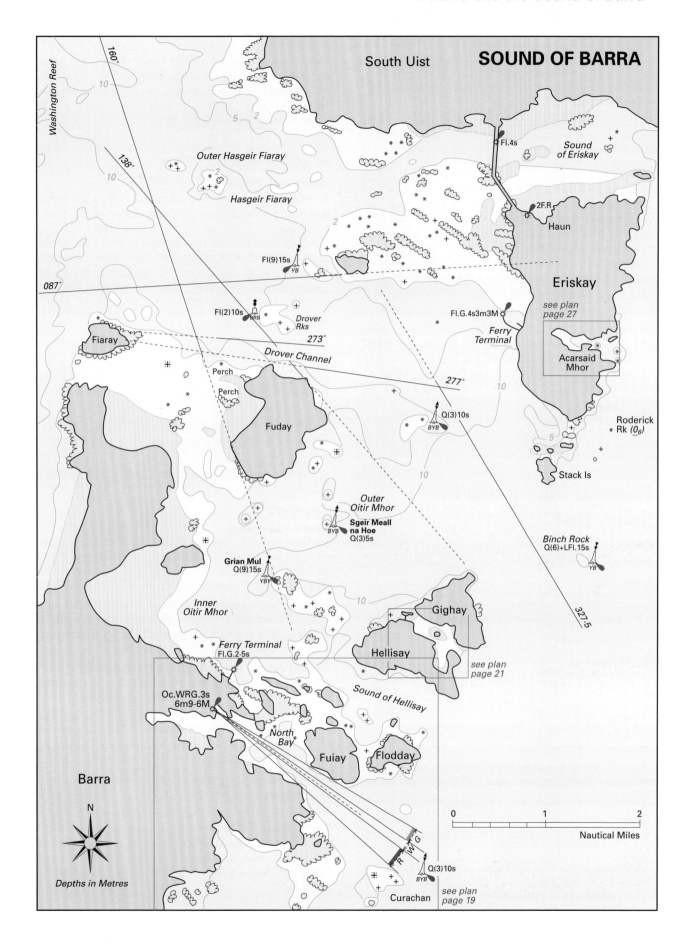

SOUND OF BARRA

South Uist

Washington Reef

160°

138°

10

10

087°

Outer Hasgeir Fiaray

Hasgeir Fiaray

2

2

Fl.4s

Sound of Eriskay

2F.R

Haun

Eriskay

Fl(9)15s
YB

Fl(2)10s
BRB

Drover Rks

273°

Drover Channel

Fl.G.4s3m3M

Ferry Terminal

277°

see plan page 27

Acarsaid Mhor

Roderick Rk *(0₆)*

Fiaray

Perch

Perch

Fuday

Q(3)10s
BYB

10

5

Stack Is

10

Outer Oitir Mhor

Sgeir Meall na Hoe
Q(3)5s
BYB

Binch Rock
Q(6)+LFl.15s
YB

Grian Mul
Q(9)15s
YBY

Inner Oitir Mhor

10

Gighay

Hellisay

327.5

Ferry Terminal
Fl.G.2·5s

Sound of Hellisay

see plan page 21

Oc.WRG.3s 6m9-6M

North Bay

Barra

Fuiay

Flodday

N

Depths in Metres

0   1   2

Nautical Miles

R W G

Q(3)10s
BYB

Curachan

see plan page 19

The northeast points of Gighay and Fuday in line 138° and the southwest points of Lingay and Eriskay in line 124° provide additional checks on position, and the current chart recommends a bearing of 150° on the summit of Fuday.

If the marks can be identified this passage will probably give an easier ride than by going outside Washington Reef.

Directions

From northwest if the marks (View A, page 24) can be identified take the passage east of Washington Reef, otherwise keep outwith the 20-metre contour until Lingay and Ben Scrien, Eriskay, have been identified, and bring them into line bearing 087°.

Keep on this line until past Fiaray then steer southeast towards the summit of Fuday until the beacons on Fiaray are in line astern 273°.

Follow round the northeast side of Fuday at a distance of about ¼ mile and steer for the northeast point of Gighay. As with all pilotage on the west side of the Outer Hebrides this depends heavily on good visibility.

Lights

Buoys and ferry terminals are lit as shown on the plan on page 25.

Passage from Barra to South Uist

Chart

2770 (1:30,000). OS map *31*

Tides

The northeast-going stream begins +0530 Ullapool (+0110 Dover)

The southwest-going stream begins −0045 Ullapool (−0505 Dover)

Constant −0032 Ullapool (−0442 Dover)

Height in metres

MHWS	MHWN	MTL	MLWN	MLWS
4·2	3·2	2·5	1·8	0·6

Dangers and marks

Curachan, Red Rocks, and Curachan east cardinal light buoy (see page 19).

Binch Rock, at a depth of 3 metres 1½ miles south of Eriskay, is marked by a south cardinal light buoy.

Galeac, 3 metres high, lies a mile north of Binch Rock buoy.

Roderick Rock, 3½ cables NNE of Galeac, dries 0·6 metre.

Hartamul, 25 metres high, lies 7 cables south of Ru Melvick, South Uist, with drying rocks up to 5 cables SSW and 2 cables northeast of it.

Directions

Pass ½ mile east of visible dangers and marks to clear those which are unseen; however, the west side of Hartamul is cleaner and it can be passed on that side. Passages closer inshore are described in relation to individual anchorages.

Acarsaid Mhor, Eriskay

Waypoint on leading line 57°03'·75N 7°16'·1W

Eriskay is a well populated island with a sheltered natural harbour on its east side. The main settlement at Haun at the north end of the island is difficult to approach through rocks and sandbanks in the Sound of Eriskay although there are light beacons for the benefit of the car ferry from South Uist; with the large-scale chart it might be possible to approach in quiet weather.

Dangers and marks

Roderick Rock, 6½ cables south of the entrance, dries 0·6 metres.

Drying rocks in the entrance are shown on the plan.

Leading lights on columns with white boards lead 285° between these rocks.

Three unlit red perches with reflective diamond topmarks mark drying reefs along the south shore.

A rock which dries 3 metres lies east of the narrowest part of the entrance, with a stbd-hand light buoy close south of it.

Approach

From south keep at least ½ mile offshore until the leading beacons are identified. Alternatively pass west of Galeac and steer to pass ½ cable east of Grey Point (Rubha Liath) taking care not to stray to the east, to avoid Roderick Rock.

On passing Rubha Liath keep Rubha Meall nan Caorach and the east point of Stack Islands open of Rubha Liath astern 210° until on the leading line to avoid the rock which dries 0·9 metre.

Approach with the leading beacons in line 285° until close to the promontory on which they stand, and pass between the perch and stbd-hand buoy.

From north pass west of Hartamul, identify the entrance by houses but keep Stack Islands open of Rubha Liath 210° until the leading beacons are in line 285° to avoid drying rocks on the north side of the entrance.

Anchorage

Visitors moorings have been laid on the south side of the harbour. Alternatively anchor as convenient clear of moorings and shoal water, but the bottom is soft mud and is reputed to be foul with old moorings. Steps are provided at the west end of the quay.

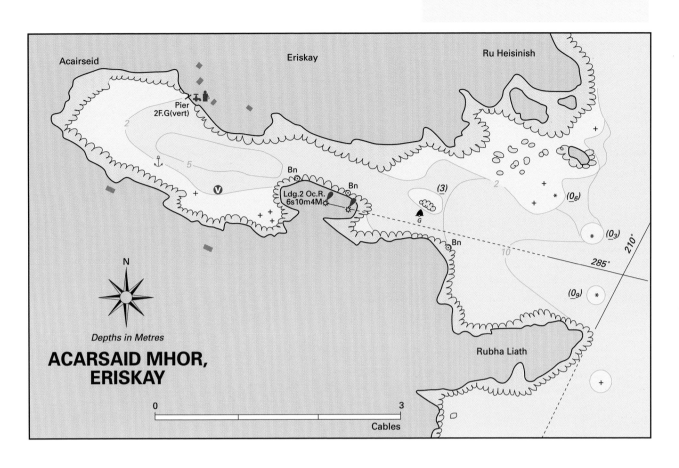

Acairseid   Eriskay   Ru Heisinish

Pier
2F.G(vert)

Bn   Bn

Ldg.2 Oc.R.
6s10m4M

(3)

G

(0₆)

Bn

(0₃)

210°

285°

10

(0₉)

N

Depths in Metres

**ACARSAID MHOR,
ERISKAY**

Rubha Liath

0   3

Cables

Approach to Acarsaid Mhor, Eriskay

Acarsaid Mhor, Eriskay

Acarsaid Mhor, Eriskay

Eriskay Sound, from SW

Sound of Eriskay

With the completion of the new causeway this looks an inviting anchorage, but much of it is shallow and there are some well-charted rocks. If a yacht can reach the pool off Haun she should be able to lie afloat at anchor in comfort.

The approach from south is straightforward; from north two detached drying rocks lie 1½ca off the north shore between Hartamul and Calvay Island. At Calvay a drying spit extends 1½ca northwest towards Calvay Rock which covers 1 metre at HW springs (is awash at HW neaps), 3ca from the island. If Calvay Rock cannot be seen, sound your way round the spit and steer west for Stag Rock beacon, about 1 mile distant and almost in line with the bridge in the middle of the causeway.

Keep Bank Rock beacon on the port bow, and when it is abeam, turn to port, pass Bank Rock beacon close on your starboard side heading southeast and come round to southwest to head just north of the church. Keep a lookout for a reef extending from the southeast shore, as well as Haun Rock in the middle of the pool, and anchor between Haun Rock and the ferry slip.

Except shoal-draught yachts, do not approach until Bank Rock is awash.

A disused ferry mooring lies NE of the slipway alignment structure.

Lights

Ldg Lts 285° Oc.R.6s 4M
Stbd-hand Lt buoy Fl.G.6s (Ra refl)
Flood lights and 2F.G(vert) at pier

At night approach on leading lights 285°, pass close south of the Fl.G light buoy and keep mid-channel in the narrows. Reflective topmarks on beacons on the south shore and the lights at the pier help at this stage. Avoid approaching at LW springs, owing to the shoal rock in the narrows.

Supplies

Shop, post office, pub/restaurant, telephone, all at Haun more than 1½ miles from the pier. Water tap, diesel (ask at shop in Haun) and rubbish containers all at pier.

II. South Uist and Benbecula

For index chart, see page 9.

Passage notes for the east shore of South Uist

Tides

Off Loch Boisdale tidal streams run at up to 2 knots off salient points

The north-going stream begins +0520 Ullapool (+0100 Dover)

The south-going stream begins −0040 Ullapool (−0500 Dover)

At Rubha Melvick a tidal eddy causes a permanent set to southwest

Dangers and marks

Clan Ewan Rock and other rocks extend ¼ mile offshore ½ mile north of Rubha na h-Ordaig, which lies 1¼ mile NNE of Ru Melvick.

McKenzie Rock, a mile north of Rubha na h-Ordaig, is marked by a red can light buoy. A rock at a depth of less than 2 metres lies ½ cable east of a direct line between Rubha na h-Ordaig and the light buoy.

Calvay Island, on the south side of the entrance to Loch Boisdale, has a white rectangular light beacon near its east end.

Stuley Island lies 3 miles north of Calvay Island, with rocks 3 cables east of it.

Usinish lighthouse, a white tower 12 metres in height, stands on a 40-metre cliff 10 miles north of Calvay Island.

Lochboisdale

Loch Boisdale

Waypoint ¼ mile NNE of Calvay light 57°08'·8N 7°15'W

Charts

2770 (1:12,500). OS map *31*

Tides

In Loch Boisdale the in-going stream begins +0530 Ullapool (+0110 Dover). The out-going stream begins –0045 Ullapool (–0505 Dover)

Constant –0045 Ullapool (–0455 Dover)

Height in metres

MHWS	MHWN	MTL	MLWN	MLWS
4·3	3·0	2·4	1·6	0·5

Dangers and marks

McKenzie Rock, ½ mile offshore ESE of the entrance, at a depth of 2·4 metres, is marked by a port-hand light buoy.

Calvay Island light beacon is a white rectangular structure. Drying rocks lie southeast and south of Calvay Island and submerged rocks lie up to 1½ cables WNW of the island.

Gasay Island, a mile WNW of Calvay Island, has a white rectangular light beacon on its northeast side. Gasay Rock, nearly a cable east of Gasay Island, dries 0·9 metre.

Sgeir Rock, on the north side of the fairway north of Gasay at a depth of 1·2 metres, is marked on its south side by a green conical light buoy.

Drying rocks at Eilean Dubh on the south side of the entrance to Bagh Dubh are marked by a black light beacon 2 metres in height SSE of the ferry terminal.

Rocks on the south side of the loch are described separately.

A stbd-hand light buoy in mid-channel N of the beacon on Gasay is of no concern to yachts.

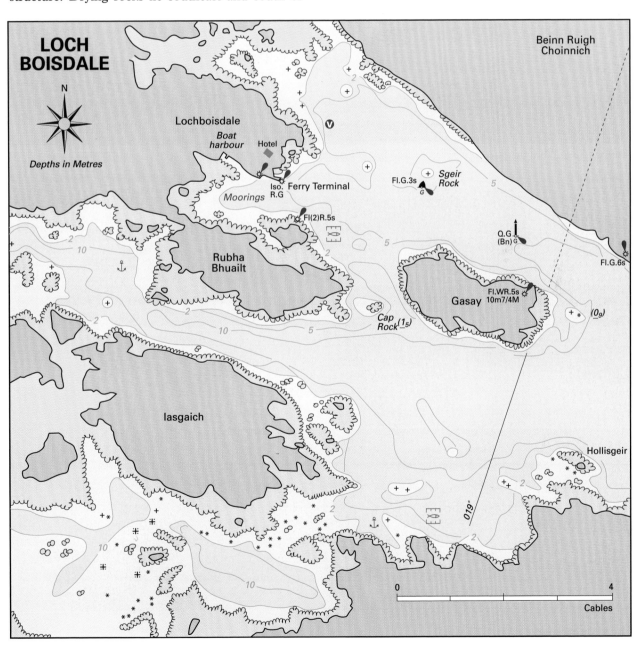

Rubha Bhuailt, Loch Boisdale

South Lochboisdale

Lights

McKenzie Rock Lt buoy Fl(3)R.15s

Calvay Island Lt bn Fl(2)WRG.10s16m7-4M, showing red over McKenzie Rock, and a narrow green sector towards submerged rocks at the north side of the entrance

Gasay Lt bn Fl.WR.5s10m7/4M shows red over Gasay Rock

Lt bn on N shore, ENE of Gasay Fl.G.6s3m3M

Stbd-hand Lt bn Q.G

Sgeir Rock Lt buoy Fl.G.3s

Ferry terminal pier head Iso.RG.4s8m2M

Ferry terminal linkspan 2F.G(vert)

Eilean Dubh Fl(2)R.5s

At night, approach in the white sector of Calvay light beacon, and in the white sector of Gasay light beacon, passing south of the Fl.G light beacon and Fl.G.3s light buoy, then head towards the lights at the pier.

Anchorages

Visitors moorings have been laid northeast of the ferry terminal.

Bagh Dubh, southwest of the ferry terminal, is surrounded by drying reefs, occupied by moorings which sometimes cause foul anchors, and the bottom is soft mud. It is best used as a temporary anchorage to go ashore for stores. Take care to avoid obstructing approach to the ferry terminal.

A fishery jetty in the northwest corner of the bay together with a breakwater, the head of which dries at chart datum, forms a boat harbour where a yacht of moderate draught might go alongside at half flood. A reef extends on the southeast side of the approach as far as the west end of the linkspan leaving a narrow channel on its northeast side. Approach on a northwest course parallel to the face of the head of the breakwater.

Shop (3 miles; tourist office can arrange taxi), post office, telephone, hotel, bank. Petrol, diesel and car hire at garage (¼ mile). Diesel expected to be available in 2004. Water at boat harbour or from a large hose at the main pier. Rubbish bins. Tourist information office and toilets and showers at boat harbour.

Rubha Bhuailt A fish cage formerly charted in this anchorage was not there in 2002, but holding has been found to be poor. In the passage from Bagh Dubh, Cap Rock which dries 1·5 metres lies in mid-channel. Keep to Gasay side of channel until the south side of Gasay is open to avoid Cap Rock.

South Lochboisdale. Submerged and drying rocks lie up to ¾ cable off the south shore east of Hollisgeir, an extensive reef part of which is just above water. The east end of Gasay under the peak of Beinn Ruigh Choinnich 019° astern leads close west of rocks west of Hollisgeir.

A ruined jetty lies 3 cables WSW of Hollisgeir, with a drying rock close northwest of it, a shoal ¾ cable north of the jetty, and a 2-metre patch 1½ cables NNE of the jetty. Fish cages lie 1 cable east of the jetty. Anchor southeast of the fish cages or northwest of the ruined jetty.

Loch Eynort

Waypoint NE of Na Dubh-sgeirean 57°13'·2N 7°15'W

A landlocked loch with a tortuous entrance in which the tide runs strongly and which should be treated with the greatest respect, although the scenery of the upper loch is worth the effort.

Charts

2825 (1:25,000). OS map *22*.

Tides

In the narrows of Sruthan Beag, tidal streams run at up to 7 knots with eddies along both sides and overfalls in the channel. The in-going stream begins –0605 Ullapool (+0200 Dover). The out-going stream begins –0010 Ullapool (–0430 Dover). Both flood and ebb tides set obliquely across Bogha Dearg when it is covered.

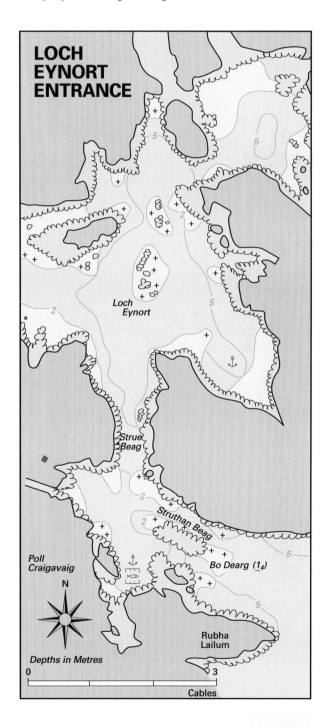

Loch Eynort, entrance from southeast

Loch Eynort, west end from SE

Constant −0045 Ullapool (−0455 Dover)

Height in metres

MHWS	MHWN	MTL	MLWN	MLWS
4·3	3·0	2·4	1·6	0·5

Dangers and marks

In the outer loch, Na Dubh-sgeirean are islets above water off Eilean nan Gamhna which lies off the south point of the entrance, with a drying reef ¼ cable northeast of them.

Bogha Carrach which dries 3·5 metres, together with a patch of submerged rocks, lie 1½ cables off-shore 4 cables WNW of Na Dubh-sgeirean. Still Rocks, 4 cables further west, dry 1·4 metres.

Bogha Coilenish, ½ cable southeast of Rubha Coilenish on the north side of the loch opposite Bogha Carrach, dries 0·5 metre.

In the narrows Bogha Dearg dries 1·4 metres. Drying rocks extend from the east side of Strue Beag.

Directions

The narrows should only be attempted at or just before high or low slack water; the deeper and cleaner passage is to the north of Bogha Dearg.

Anchorage

Anchor anywhere in the inner loch clear of rocks and fish cages, and in Poll Craigavaig at the narrows, but this is rather restricted by fish cages.

Bay northeast of Strue Beag is reported to be very soft mud. Better holding in Bagh Lathaich off wooden shed.

Occasional anchorage in the outer loch on sand at Cearcdal Bay, in the southwest corner.

Hidden Harbour (Acarsaid Fhalach)

57°20'N 7°13'W

A very occasional anchorage about ¾ mile south of Ornish Island which lies in the mouth of Loch Skipport. The following notes are provided by Captain Macleod, and the plan is part of an old chart with soundings in fathoms. Note that the current chart shows several submerged rocks northeast of the entrance.

The inlet is difficult to discern from seaward and care must be taken to identify the entrance before making an approach. Rubha Rossel, south of Hidden Harbour is a prominent rounded hillock darker in colour than the surrounding landscape.

Note Rubha Rossel is shown as Russel Pt. on the plan, and En Cireach as Caray I.

Directions

Approaching from the south identify Rubha Rossel and steer midway between it and En Cireach, keeping the eastern extremity of Ornish Island open east of the eastern extremity of En Cireach 350°.

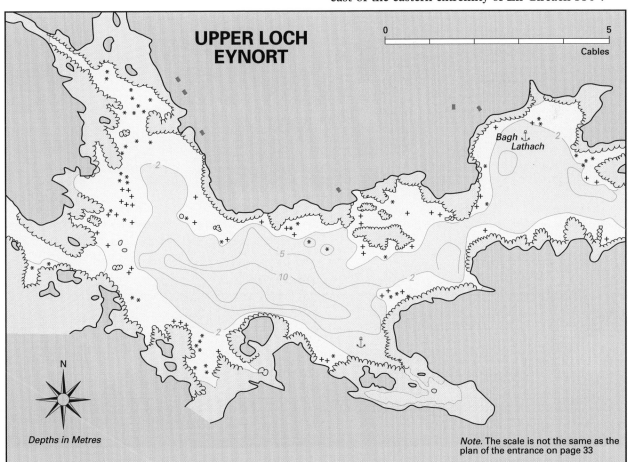

UPPER LOCH EYNORT

Cables

Bagh Lathach

N

Depths in Metres

Note. The scale is not the same as the plan of the entrance on page 33

Loch Eynort, east end of upper loch

Hidden Harbour (South Uist)

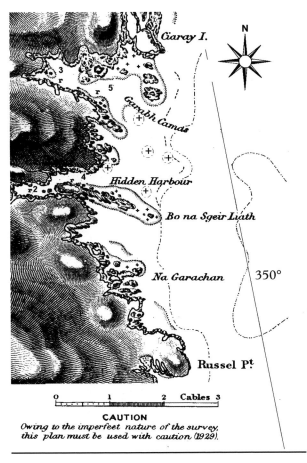

CAUTION

Owing to the imperfect nature of the survey, this plan must be used with caution (1929).

Hidden Harbour

Approaching from north steer for Rubha Rossel keeping a minimum of 2 cables offshore to avoid foul ground to the north of Bo na Sgeir Liath, with Ornish Island open east of En Cireach astern 350°, as above.

Midway between En Cireach and Rubha Rossel look for a break in the coastline with a small shingle beach in the northwest corner of the main entrance. Bo na Sgeir Liath covers about half tide, and is usually identifiable; keeping slightly to the north of this rock while heading for the shingle beach will take you into the main entrance. The shingle beach has been found difficult to identify at LW, being hidden behind a skerry.

There is plenty of water close in to the south shore of the main entrance. Just before the shingle beach, the channel turns southwards and narrows. At the first turn keep mid-channel with a tendency towards the north shore, to avoid a drying rock in the entrance to the small inlet to port. Once inside the harbour, boats can tie up to a rock shelf on the north side but care must be taken on a falling tide that there is adequate water under the keel at all times.

Loch Skipport

Waypoint ¼ mile NE of Ornish 57°20'N 7°13'W

A popular, well sheltered and easily entered loch in spectacular surroundings under the slopes of Hecla.

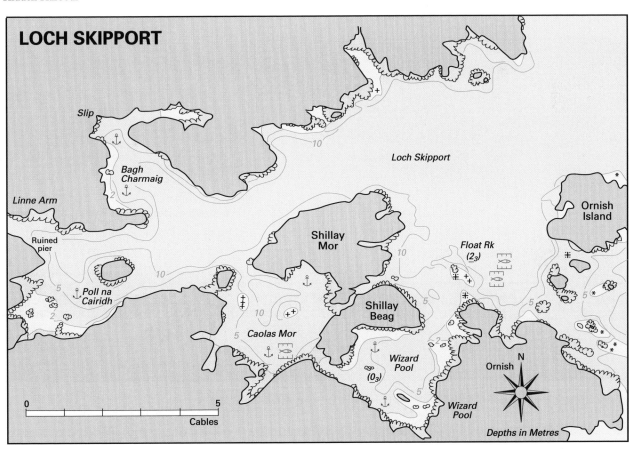

Loch Skipport, approach to Wizard Pool from NNE. Float Rock lies right of centre

Loch Skipport from east side of Wizard Pool; Wizard Island in foreground and Caolas Mor beyond

Charts

2904 (1:25,000), *2825* (1:12,500). OS map *22*

Tides

Tidal streams are slight except in narrow channels, including the entrance to Linne Arm. The in-going stream begins +0545 Ullapool (+0125 Dover). The out-going stream begins –0035 Ullapool (–0455 Dover)

Constant –0052 Ullapool (–0602 Dover)

Height in metres

MHWS	MHWN	MTL	MLWN	MLWS
4·6	3·3	2·5	1·7	0·5

Anchorages

Wizard Pool is the first anchorage on the south side. Float Rock, between Shillay Mor and Ornish, dries 2·3 metres, and fish cages lie east of the rock. To avoid Float Rock steer towards Shillay Mor until within a cable of that island.

Pass the east end of Shillay Beag to the west of mid-channel to avoid drying rocks off Ornish and then pass closer to Wizard Island to avoid a drying rock east of the south end of Shillay Beag.

Anchor anywhere around the sides of the pool. Very soft holding S of Wizard Island. Water may be had from a burn south of Wizard Island.

The bay on the southeast side of Shillay Beag provides some shelter from northeasterly swell; in southerly gales fierce gusts come down from Hecla.

Caolas Mor, otherwise known as Little Kettle Pool, has submerged rocks at a depth of about 1 metre in the middle and others on the west side, about 0·3 metre, and fish cages on its south side.

The pool can be entered from the west, or by the narrow channel from Wizard Pool, but a depth of only 1·3 metres is shown on the chart at the south side of the west end of this channel.

Bagh Charmaig on the north side of the loch to the west of Shillay Mor has a bottom of soft mud.

Poll na Cairidh in the southwest corner of the loch has drying rocks more than a cable from the shore but they are easily avoided by keeping outwith the 5-metre line; this bay has been found to provide excellent shelter in a southerly gale.

Linne Arm is virtually landlocked but the surroundings are less shut in by hills. The bottom in Linne Arm is stony and the holding may not be good; anchor chain will be noisy in unsettled weather. The pier at the entrance is ruined and there are extensive fish cages on the south shore with a new slip from which they are serviced; water might be had there. A phone box stands ¼ mile from the slip.

Caolas Luirsay, a channel on the west side of Luirsay Dubh at the north entrance to Loch Skipport, can be entered from south or by a narrow channel from northeast, but is affected by swell in northerly winds. A submerged rock at the north end of the pool extends over a considerable area and is best passed on its east side (see photo page 40).

Loch Sheilavaig, ½ mile west of Caolas Luirsay, is a rather featureless loch with many fish cages, but it is full of rocks and provides an interesting challenge.

Wizard Pool, Loch Skipport, South Uist

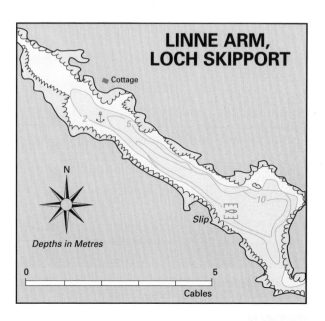

Poll na Cairidh, Loch Skipport

Caolas Luirsay from ENE with entrance to Loch Sheilavaig at upper right. Eilean an Fraoch Mia is beyond the right-hand edge of the photo. Rocks in Caolas Luirsay show clearly

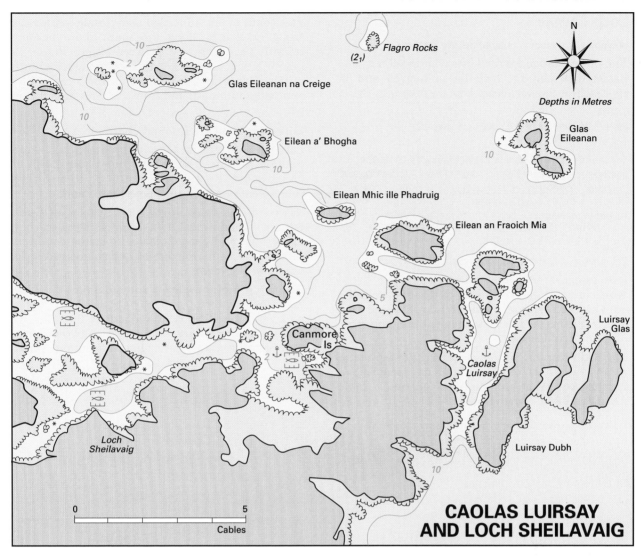

**CAOLAS LUIRSAY
AND LOCH SHEILAVAIG**

The fish farm operators regard the loch as their private property.

The entrance, between Eilean Mhic ille Phadruig and Eilean an Fraoich Mia, is most easily found by taking a bearing astern on Glas-Eileanan (062°). Pass about 50 metres west of Canmore Island so as to pass east of a drying rock ½ cable from the island as well as a shallow rocky patch which extends almost to the west shore of the narrows, and anchor south of the island.

Passage notes – South Uist to North Uist

Chart *2904*

Tides

The north-going stream begins +0550 Ullapool (+0130 Dover)

The south-going stream begins –0010 Ullapool (–0430 Dover) at a spring rate of 1h knots off salient points

Dangers and marks

The principal landmarks are the hills: Hecla (606m) on South Uist, Beinn a' Tuath, Wiay (102m), Beinn a' Charnain, Ronay (115m), and Eaval (347m) on North Uist, conspicuously wedge-shaped from east, provide some guide as to position.

A landfall buoy (RW pillar, 57°22'·3N 7°11'·4W) lies in the mouth of Bagh nam Faoileann between South Uist and Wiay.

The power station at Loch Carnan, a long rectangular building with two chimneys, is conspicuous.

Greanamul Deas, a prominent islet 10 metres high is 6 cables north of the northeast point of Wiay; Bo Greanamul with a depth of 2·1 metres lies 4 cables ESE of Greanamul Deas. Luirsay Glas, well open of Wiay 193°, leads east of Bo Greanamul. Greanamul Deas should be distinguished from Greanamul, about 2 miles further north.

Ritchie Rock (**Waypoint** ¼ mile E of rock 57°28'·3N 7°09'W) lies 3½ cables off the east side of Ronay at a depth of 0·6 metre. Rueval, a prominent hill on Benbecula, 123 metres high, open south of Rubha na Rodagrich 263°, leads south of Ritchie Rock, and Madadh Mor, off the entrance to Loch Maddy, open east of Floddaymore 013° leads close east of it.

Loch Carnan

Waypoint S of landfall buoy 57°22'·2N 7°11'·4W

The power station for the Uists with its oil terminal stands here and the loch has a buoyed and lit approach. A few yachts are kept on moorings there.

Charts
2904 (1:25,000), *2825* (1:12,500). OS map *22*

Tides
The in-going stream begins +0535 Ullapool (+0115 Dover)
The out-going stream begins –0025 Ullapool (–0445 Dover)
Constant –0020 Ullapool (–0440 Dover) at springs; –0110 Ullapool (–0530 Dover) at neaps
Height in metres

MHWS	MHWN	MTL	MLWN	MLWS
4·5	3·2	2·6	1·9	0·7

Directions for the passage south of Gasay

It is essential to identify each island correctly to avoid various hazards. The key to this passage is the most southerly islet on the north side of the passage, 3 metres in height and well separated from the other islets south of Gasay.

The main hazards are a rock which dries 0·6 metre a cable northeast of Glas-Eilean na Creig and a submerged rock at a depth of 1·2 metres, a cable southwest of the 3-metre islet.

Pass south of Glas-Eileanan and ¼ mile outside the string of islands along the south shore heading towards Gasay, to pass between Flagro Rocks, ½ mile WNW of Glas-Eileanan, and drying reefs north of Glas-Eilean na Creig. Steer for the 3-metre islet and pass south of it, and from there towards the oil wharf.

Directions for the buoyed channel

Landfall buoy provides useful confirmation of one's position. Identify Outer No.1 buoy lying north of Grey Island Rocks, pass north of it and pass subsequent buoys on the appropriate hand.

Approaching from north keep 2 cables off Dubh Sgeir a' Tuath and Dubh Sgeir a' Deas, each 1 metre high and lying 2 cables from the southeast shore of Wiay, to avoid drying and submerged rocks to seaward of them.

Anchor clear of the fairway and moorings; the inlets west and southwest of Direy are beset by drying rocks, but space can be found among them further from the relatively industrial surroundings. Moorings for visitors have been laid south of Direy.

Loch Carnan from ESE. The power station and the quays are on the left. The rock lower left of centre is the drying rock WNW of the '3-metre islet'

Loch Carnan from W

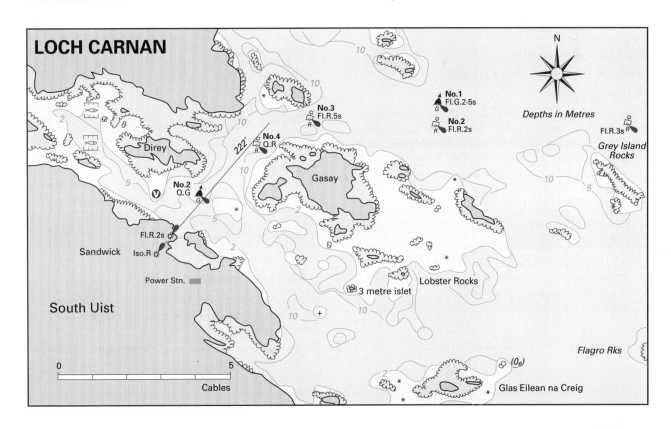

LOCH CARNAN

No.1
Fl.G.2·5s

No.2
Fl.R.2s

Depths in Metres

Fl.R.3s

Grey Island Rocks

No.3
Fl.R.5s

222°

No.4
Q.R

Direy

Gasay

No.2
Q.G

Fl.R.2s

Sandwick   Iso.R

Power Stn.

South Uist

Lobster Rocks

3 metre islet

0   5

Cables

Flagro Rks

(0₆)

Glas Eilean na Creig

Peter's Port from SSE

Lights

Landfall buoy LFl.10s
Outer *No.1* Fl.R.3s
Inner No.1 Fl.G.2·5s
No.2 Fl.R.2s
No.3 Fl.R.5s
Ldg Lts 222° *Front* Fl.R.2s7m
Rear Iso.R.10s11m5M
No.4 Q.R
No.2 Q.G (green conical)

At night follow the buoyed channel.

Supplies

Diesel and water are available at the oil terminal wharf; ask at office on the wharf. The oil terminal wharf is a piled construction, but concrete dolphins a short distance to the west may be easier to go alongside. These have rather insecure ladders.

Phone box by derelict cottage 100 metres up track from pier.

Benbecula anchorages

For a small shoal-draught boat a fascinating network of inner channels extends over a distance of about 10 miles from south to north.

Charts

2904 (1:25,000) gives as much detail for many of these anchorages as could be provided by a pilot, so it is not duplicated here except where additional detail can be shown, and that chart should be carried. The obsolete fathoms chart 3168, a fine 19th-century engraving shows some further detail (see Appendix I). OS map 22.

Tides

Constant −0052 Ullapool (−0602 Dover)
Height in metres

MHWS	MHWN	MTL	MLWN	MLWS
4·6	3·3	2·5	1·7	0·5

Peter's Port

57°23'·4N 7°14'·4W

The remote and isolated quay was built at Peter's Port earlier this century because the mainland authorities were unable to agree whether to build a new quay to serve communities further north or further south; so they built it in the middle of nowhere. A modern slip has been added and it now serves local fishermen.

Dangers and marks

Beinn a' Tuath on Wiay, the highest hill on the east shore between South Uist and Ronay, lies NNE of the entrance.

Dubh-sgeir a' Tuath and Dubh-sgeir a' Deas, both 1 metre high, lie about 2 cables SE of Wiay, with drying and submerged rocks to seaward of them.

Peter's Port from WSW

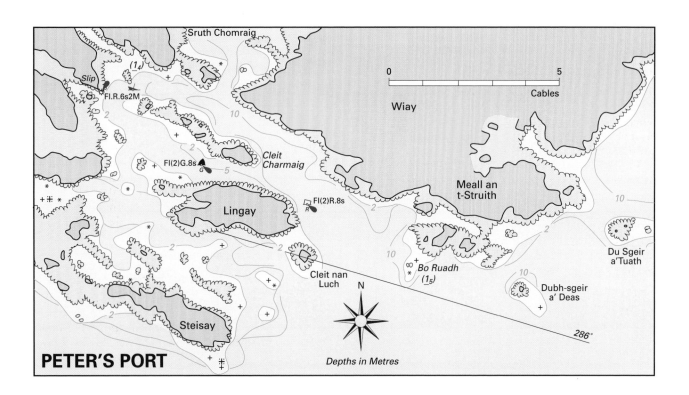

Bogha Ruadh, a drying rock at the east side of the entrance, lies a cable southwest of a group of islets and reefs south of Wiay and Cleit nan Luch is a small islet on the west side of the entrance.

The channel north of Lingay is marked by two light buoys.

A wreck lies close southeast of the rock which dries 1·4 metres about a cable ENE of the slip; on older charts the wreck is shown further SE and it would be unwise to pass west and north of the rocks west of Cleit Charmaig even if the wreck is uncovered, without careful investigation.

A reef lies parallel with the south face of the slip and 15 metres from it. The slip is marked at its outer end by a light beacon.

Directions

Approaching from north keep 2 cables off both Dubh Sgeir rocks, to avoid drying and submerged rocks to seaward of them.

The south tangent of Lingay open south of Cleit nan Luch 286° clears Bogha Ruadh.

Pass north of Cleit nan Luch and Lingay and south of Cleit Charmaig and anchor as convenient clear of the approach to the slip which is used by fishing boats.

Sruth Chomhraig, on the north side of Peter's Port, is lined with fish cages on its west side and drying rocks on the east side.

Lights
Port-hand buoy Fl(2)R.8s
Stbd-hand buoy Fl(2)G.8s
Bn at slip Fl.R.6s2M

Supplies and services
None. Phone about 3 miles.

Loch a' Laip

Waypoint ENE of Rubha Cam na Gall 57°24'·8N 7°10'·6W

Identify Greanamul Deas and keep clear of Bo Greanamul (*Passage notes* above, page 41) and pass north of Bo' Carrach heading 230° for the south shore to avoid rocks on the north side of the entrance.

A submerged rock north of the drying rock in the mouth of Bagh a' Bhraoige is avoided by keeping Rubha Cam nan Gall open north of the unnamed point 3 cables west of it 090°.

There are fish cages in several parts of the loch, in particular in Bagh a' Bhraoige, formerly the most suitable anchorage; otherwise there is nothing to add to the information on the chart.

Loch Keiravagh

A more straightforward loch, ¼ mile north of Loch a' Laip. As well as the obvious drying rocks, note submerged rocks as shown on the chart on either side of the entrance.

Loch a'Laip from ENE

Scarilode Bay, Loch Uskavagh

Loch Uskavagh

Waypoint ½ mile south of Greanamul 57°26'·5N 7°10'·7W

Chart

A very old chart, *1154* shows greater detail – subject to the usual caution about using old charts.

Notes Greanamul should not be confused with Greamnamul Deas, 2 miles further south. It may not be possible to identify the 'white house' shown on the chart, and the approach is best made at low tide when some of the most hazardous rocks show.

Sgeir na Geadh at the north side of the narrows is fairly easy to identify; approach with Sgeir na Geadh bearing 270°.

Once through the narrows the tangents of Orasay Uskavagh and Maaey Riabhach on the south side of the loch in line astern 105° lead clear of hidden dangers.

Neavag Bay on the north side of the loch is well sheltered but the bottom is very soft mud.

Other anchorages can be found in moderate depths around the shores of the main part of the loch.

Kallin

Waypoint ½ mile ESE of Rubha na Rodagrich 57°27'·9N 7°10'·0W

A small community principally occupied with lobster fishing; working in summer on the Atlantic coast. Smaller boats from Kallin pass regularly under a bridge in the causeway at North Ford, which has a headroom of 2·4 metres.

Tides

The in-going stream begins +0535 Ullapool (+0115 Dover)
The out-going stream begins –0025 Ullapool (–0445 Dover)
Constant –0040 Ullapool (–0500 Dover)
Height in metres

MHWS	MHWN	MTL	MLWN	MLWS
4·8	3·6	2·8	1·9	0·7

Dangers and marks

Bogha Mor, 4 cables SSW of Rubha na Rodagrich, the south point of Ronay, dries 3 metres, and Morrison's Rock lies 3 cables ESE of Bogha Mor at a depth of 2·8 metres.

Other drying rocks lie 2 cables south and southwest of Rubha na Monach, the southwest point of Ronay, and drying reefs extend ½ cable southwest of that point.

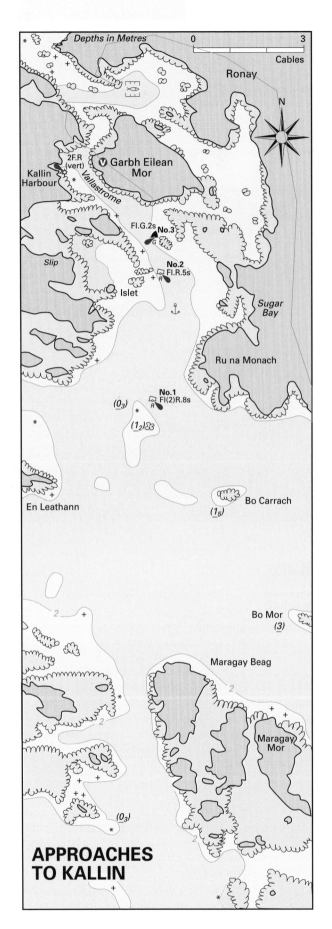

APPROACHES
TO KALLIN

Light buoys mark the approach channel to the harbour.

Directions

From south keep the summit of Beinn a' Tuath open of the east side of Greanamul astern 200° to clear Morrison's Rock. Turn to pass 1 cable off the south points of Ronay to avoid the detached drying rocks and the reef southwest of Rubha na Monach. Pass northeast of No.1 red can light buoy.

Alternatively pass west of the Maragay islands, but note the various submerged and drying rocks on the west side of the passage. Head to pass close to the east end of Eilean Leathann, to avoid a submerged rock lying a cable east of that island.

From north keep ½ mile off the east side of Ronay to avoid Ritchie's Rock (for clearing marks see *Passage notes* above, page 41) and pass a cable south of Ronay as above.

Pass midway between *No.1* red can light buoy and islets off St Michael's Point to port to clear the drying rock SW of that buoy.

Vallastrome, the channel north of Gairbh-Eilean Beag; has drying rocks on both sides, marked by light buoys. A conspicuous white cottage open northeast of Gairbh-Eilean Beag 309° leads between these rocks, and after passing No.3 buoy on the starboard hand keep in mid-channel. The tide runs strongly in Vallastrome and care is needed when manoeuvring.

Lights

No.1 light buoy Fl(2)R.8s
No.2 light buoy Fl.R.5s
No.3 light buoy Fl.G.2s
Harbour entrance, southeast side, 2F.R(vert)

Anchorages

Anchor in the basin between Ronay and Grimsay, clear of the fairway to the harbour.

Shoal-draught yachts, and others at neaps, anchor in a pool north of the islet which lies north of St Michael's Point (upper left on lower photo on page 49); pass 20 metres northeast of the islet to avoid the drying reef which extends south from Gairbh-Eilean Beag. Land at a slip WNW of the islet.

In easterly winds, yachts can anchor close to Ronay in the mouth of Sugar Bay.

A small harbour lies in the southwest corner of Vallastrome, yachts can moor on the northeast face of the wall outside the harbour, where the depth is 2·4 metres. Extensive submerged and drying rocks lie to the east of this berth.

The harbour itself is very small and often becomes full to capacity and a yacht is unlikely to be able to remain overnight, but it is a useful source of water and fuel. Depth inside the harbour is 2·5 metres and 1·7 metres in the entrance.

There is a single visitors buoy in Vallastrome, and it is also possible to anchor there, but the tide runs strongly and the fairway must not be obstructed.

Kallin approaches. Vallastrome is at upper right centre and Sugar Bay, Ronay, in the foreground

Kallin from Ronay. The pool north of St Michael's Point is at upper left, and Vallastrome upper right

Kallin approaches, Vallastrome

Supplies

Water tap at harbour. Diesel at harbour, enquire locally but don't expect anyone to be waiting to serve you. Yachts are supplied as a favour, although the fishermen are far too courteous to make you aware of this. Limited fishermen's chandlery. Mains electricity outlet at harbour. Travelling shop twice weekly. Live lobsters may be available. Telephone nearby.

Flodday Sound

Waypoint ¼ mile SE of Flodday More 57°29'·5N 7°09'·0W

Many possible anchorages lie in this sound and in Bagh na Caiplich just to the south.

Kallin Harbour from W

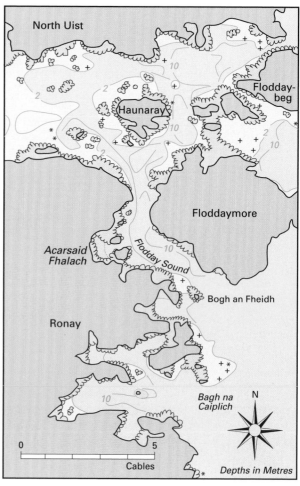

Directions

Approaching from south keep ½ mile off Ronay to avoid Ritchie Rock (for clearing marks see *Passage notes* above, page 41). Enter by the channel southwest of Floddaymore. The tide runs briskly in Flodday Sound.

Anchorages

Acarsaid Fhalach on the west side of the sound can be entered through a narrow steep-sided channel between the two islets at the entrance, and there appears (from a brief visit) to be clear depth and swinging room within. Although the current chart shows the entrance to be blocked by drying rocks, the previous chart showed depths of 2 fathoms there, and this appears to be correct. The bottom is very soft mud as there is no scour to disturb it, and there may be the odd brick.

Anchorages east of Haunaray are reasonably straightforward to approach but, at low tide, two submerged rocks in the passage southeast of Haunaray could be a hazard.

Fishing boats use the channel north of Floddaybeg but a rock in the middle of its west end just dries, and submerged rocks lie further west.

Entrance to Flodday Sound from southeast; Acarsaid Fhalach is at top left

Hidden Harbour (Acarsaid Fhalach), Flodday Sound

III. North Uist and the Sound of Harris

For the crossing from Mull and the mainland see Chapter I.

North Uist

Tides

The north-going stream begins –0550 Ullapool (+0215 Dover)

The south-going stream begins +0035 Ullapool (–0345 Dover) at a spring rate of 2 knots off salient points

Dangers

The coast is free from hidden dangers.

Bagh Moraig (Moireag Harbour)

Waypoint ¼ mile east of entrance 57°30'·9N 7°08'·4W

A remote landlocked pool with a tortuous entrance channel the outer part of which is clean, with a drying sill at the inner end, all shown reasonably clearly on the Admiralty chart.

The sill dries completely, the highest part being around the middle, which dries about 1·6 metres. The deepest water is on the south side, with at least 2 metres, 2½ hours either side of HWS. The tide runs strongly over this sill.

Most of the pool is more than 12 metres deep, with a bottom of soft mud, but it shoals towards the narrows leading to the inner pool. Moderate depths for anchoring may be found in the west third of the main pool. Excellent mussels may be found at the mouth of a burn at the head of the bay, as a reward for negotiating the entrance.

Bagh Moraig, from E

Loch Eport

Waypoint ¼ mile east of the narrows 57°33'·5N 7°07'·5W

Eaval, the wedge-shaped hill 347 metres high, lies 1½ miles south of the entrance.

Charts

2825 (1:15,000)

The current edition does not cover the head of the loch and that section of the plan here is taken from a 19th-century edition, together with a survey by the Brathay Exploration Group. OS map *18*.

Tides

The in-going stream begins +0550 Ullapool (+0130 Dover)

The out-going stream begins –0020 Ullapool (–0440 Dover)

The spring rate in the narrows is 3 knots

Constant –0040 Ullapool (–0500 Dover)

Height in metres

MHWS	MHWN	MTL	MLWN	MLWS
4·8	3·6	2·8	1·9	0·7

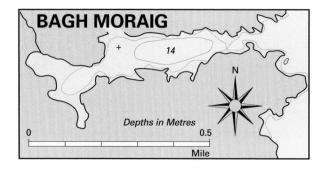

BAGH MORAIG

+ 14

N

Depths in Metres

0   0.5

Mile

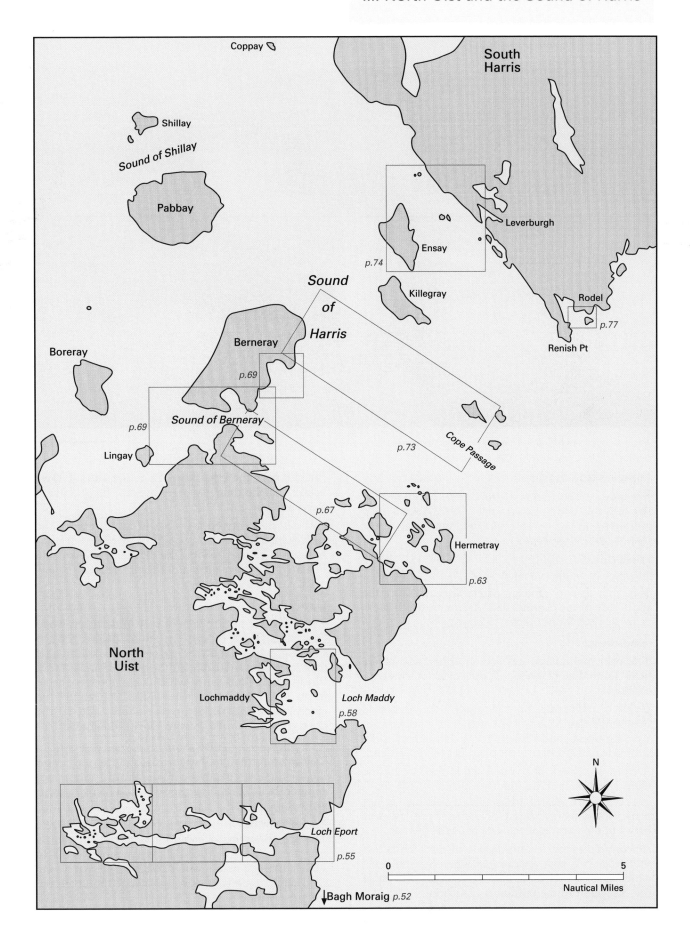

Coppay

South Harris

Shillay

Sound of Shillay

Pabbay

Sound
of
Harris

Ensay

p.74

Leverburgh

Killegray

Rodel

p.77

Renish Pt

Boreray

Berneray

p.69

p.69

Sound of Berneray

Cope Passage

p.73

Lingay

p.67

Hermetray

p.63

North
Uist

Lochmaddy

Loch Maddy

p.58

Loch Eport

p.55

N

↓Bagh Moraig *p.52*

0   5

Nautical Miles

Bagh Moraig from SW at low tide showing the drying sill   *R Arnold*

Dangers and marks

Bo Lea, 2 metres high, stands on the south side of the entrance with drying rocks further west. The entrance channel is clean but the inner parts of the loch are full of rocks.

Directions

The north point of the entrance just open of McCalter Island (Eilean Mhic Shealtair) on the south side of the channel 082° astern clears all rocks as far as One Stone Rock.

Anchorages

The principal anchorages are on either side of the loch immediately west of the narrow entrance channel.

Bagh a' Bhiorain on the south side is entered between Riffag Mhor, at the west end of which lies a drying wreck, and Riffag Beag, a drying reef at the west side of the entrance with an islet on its east end.

A cairn on a rock near the head of the bay in line with a white boulder on the hillside 129° leads between these obstructions, but if this line is not seen pass close northeast of Riffag Beag. Anchor between the cairn and the east shore of the bay.

Acarsaid Lee on the north side of the loch is less sheltered. It is best approached when Sgeir n' Iolla which dries 4 metres, about 1¼ cable southwest of the east point of the entrance, is showing.

A rock drying 2·7 metres stands at the south end of a reef which extends ½ cable south from the shore northeast of Deer Island.

Anchor near the east shore, or either side of Deer Island. The holding has been found to be poor, with weed and soft mud.

A small inlet entered a couple of cables east of the rock which dries 4m, south of the entrance to Acarsaid Lee, marked on the old chart as Acarsaid Fhalach, may have attractions for a yacht of shallow draft.

Upper loch

To go further up the loch is best undertaken when One Stone Rock (covers 2½ hours before HW) is showing, when it may be passed on its south side; then keep about ½ cable off the south shore as far as Eilean Fhearghuis, after which keep about ½ cable from the north side, and note especially the extensive drying rocks on the south side of the channel about a mile west of Eilean Fhearguis.

A drying reef extends south from the east end of Steisay more than halfway across the channel. After Steisay there are patches with depths of 1 metre, but apparently no submerged rocks, in the fairway as far as Locheport pier.

Anchor northeast of Eilean a'Cairidh in 4 metres. The area between Eilean a'Cairidh and the pier is reported to be now too shallow for most yachts to anchor there. The bottom is soft mud so that a long keel yacht would sink in; care is needed to dig in the anchor securely.

Other anchorages may be found with chart *2825*, although it does not cover the head of the loch.

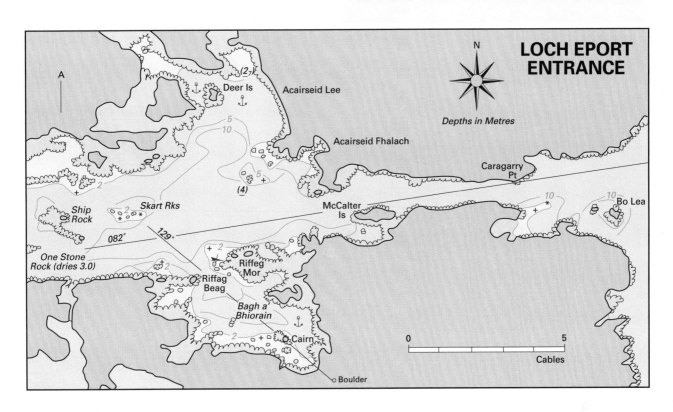

LOCH EPORT ENTRANCE

Depths in Metres

A

Deer Is

(2)

Acairseid Lee

Acairseid Fhalach

Caragarry Pt

10

10 Bo Lea

5

10

(4)

5

McCalter Is

Ship Rock

2 Skart Rks

082° 129°

One Stone Rock (dries 3.0)

2

Riffeg Mor

Riffag Beag

Bagh a' Bhiorain

Cairn

2

Boulder

0 — 5 Cables

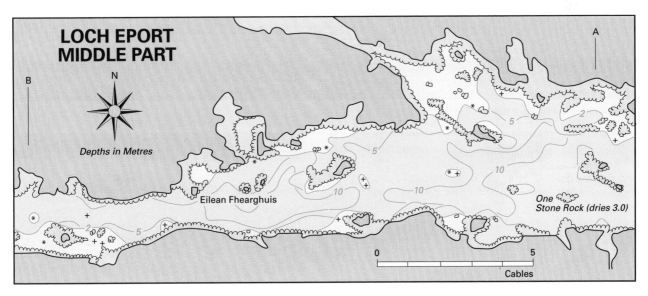

LOCH EPORT MIDDLE PART

B

N

A

Depths in Metres

5 2

5

10

10

10

One Stone Rock (dries 3.0)

Eilean Fhearghuis

2

5

0 — 5 Cables

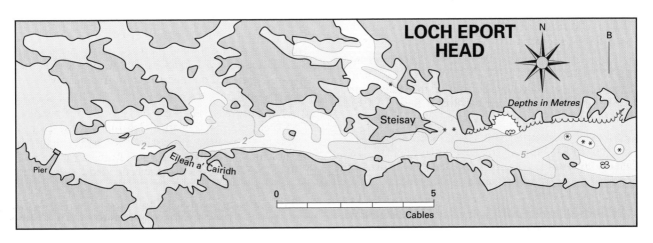

LOCH EPORT HEAD

N B

Depths in Metres

Steisay

2 2

5

Pier

Eilean a' Cairidh

0 — 5 Cables

Loch Eport entrance from NE

Loch Eport head and pier

Supplies

Shop, PO at Clachan, 1 mile west from pier. Mermaid Fish, just past the shop, supplies peat-smoked salmon. Hotel 1½ miles north from the pier.

Loch Maddy

Waypoint ¼ mile 57°36'N 7°06'W

A broad loch littered with islands and rocks but well marked and lit for the needs of car ferries. Loch Maddy is identified by the gap in the hills at the entrance, and the conspicuous angular islets, Madadh Mor and Madadh Gruamach on the south side of the entrance and Madadh Beag on the north side, as well as the small light beacon on Weaver's Point at the north point of the entrance.

Chart

2825 (1:12,500). OS map *18*

Tides

The in-going stream begins +0555 Ullapool (+0135 Dover)

The out-going stream begins –0025 Ullapool (–0445 Dover) Owing to the influence of the tidal streams along the coast, the in-going stream turns to run northeast between Weaver's Point and Madadh Beag, and the out-going stream sets strongly along the south shore.

Constant –0040 Ullapool (–0500 Dover)

Height in metres

MHWS	MHWN	MTL	MLWN	MLWS
4·8	3·6	2·8	1·9	0·7

Approach

Heavy seas may be encountered off the entrance when wind and tide are opposed, especially close to either point, and it is best to approach in mid-channel.

Dangers and marks

Submerged rocks extend ½ cable northeast from the south point of the entrance – to be taken account of if sailing inside Madadh Mor.

A small white light beacon stands on Weaver's Point, the north side of the entrance. Other light beacons are inconspicuous and are little use as daymarks.

Glas Eilean Mor, within the south side of the entrance, has drying reefs up to a cable off its west side.

Faihore and Ruigh Liath lie about a mile west of Glas Eilean Mor with reefs all round them. An unlit red buoy lies northwest of Faihore.

The main fairway is south of these islets and an unlit red perch stands at the outer edge of reefs off the south shore of the loch.

Loch Maddy entrance from southwest; Ardmaddy Bay in foreground

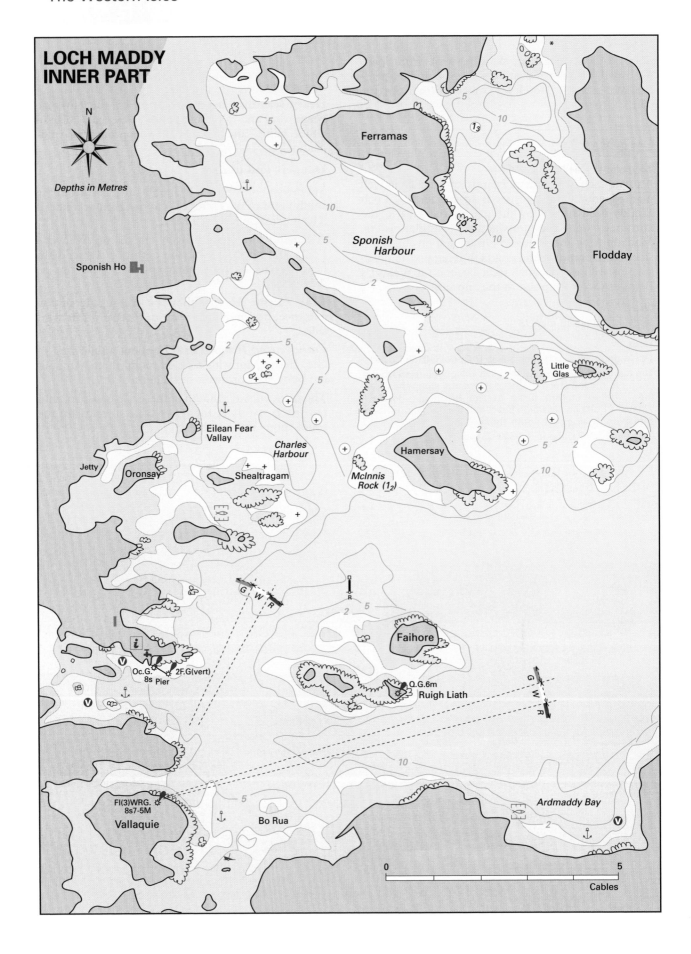

LOCH MADDY
INNER PART

N

Depths in Metres

Sponish Ho

Ferramas

Sponish
Harbour

Flodday

Little
Glas

Eilean Fear
Vallay

Charles
Harbour

Hamersay

Jetty

Oronsay

Shealtragam

McInnis
Rock (1₂)

Faihore

Oc.G.
8s Pier

2F.G(vert)

Q.G.6m
Ruigh Liath

Fl(3)WRG.
8s7-5M

Vallaquie

Bo Rua

Ardmaddy Bay

0   Cables   5

Directions

For the anchorage at the ferry terminal, pass either south, or not less than a cable north, of Glas Eilean Mor and either south of Ruigh Liath or north of the red buoy which lies northwest of Faihore.

Lights

Weaver's Point Lt Bn Fl.3s24m7M
Glas Eilean Mor Fl(2)G.4s8m5M
Ardmaddy Point LtBn Fl.R.4s7m5M
Ruigh Liath Lt bn Q.G.6m
Vallaquie Island Lt Bn Fl(3)WRG.8s11m7-5M
Ferry terminal Ldg Lts 298° *Front* 2F.G(vert)8m4M
Rear Oc.G.8s10m4M 284°-vis-304°

Anchorages

Visitors moorings are provided: two in Ardmaddy Bay, two west of the ferry terminal, four south of the island west of the terminal, and two off the east end of Oronsay.

Anchoring is prohibited east of a line through the seaward face of the twin dolphins (concrete towers) at the outer end of the linkspan. This line continues southward through the easternmost line of visitors' moorings. Ground chains lie in a north-south alignment for the more northerly moorings, and east-west for the southerly pair.

Holding ground for anchoring at the pier is poor, and yachts must leave space for ferries to manoeuvre.

Landing at concrete steps west of the linkspan. The 'Wee Pier' at Oronsay is tidal.

Services and supplies

Shops, post office, telephone, bank, hotel, doctor. Petrol and diesel at pier, water hose at pier, and at the Wee Pier inside Oronsay. Calor Gas (ask at tourist office). Sports centre, arts centre/café. Taxi/mini-bus. Showers/ baths may be had at various charges and levels of amenity at the hotel, youth hostel and sports centre. Piermaster (VHF Ch 12) ☎ 01876 500337.

Other anchorages in Loch Maddy

Ardmaddy Bay (Bagh Aird nam Madadh) on the south shore tends to be squally in southerly winds. Fish cages there had been removed at time of writing. MOD mooring buoy (frequently used by yachts).

Vallaquie, 4 cables SSE of ferry terminal. An old large MOD mooring buoy lies in the middle of the bay northeast of Vallaquie Island, with Bo Rua, which dries 0·8 metre, to the east of it.

A wreck which covers, and two drying rocks, lie towards the head of the bay; there is space to anchor between the mooring buoy and the wreck, but a submerged reef extends a cable north from the east end of Vallaquie, and fish cages lie at the west side of the bay.

Oronsay Island, about ½ mile north of the ferry pier, shelters a pool which almost dries with a stone jetty where local boats have moorings; fishing boats are often working the Atlantic coast in the summer and visitors may be invited to use a mooring. Approach by the north of Shealtragam and between Eilean Fear Valley and Oronsay. Water at the Wee Pier.

Loch Maddy from south; Faihore and Ruigh Liath left of centre

Lochmaddy Pier from W

Loch Maddy

Charles Harbour (Acarsaid Nighean Thearlaich on the chart), northwest of Hamersay, is obstructed by drying and submerged rocks, and much of the bottom is either rock or soft mud; fish cages have currently been moved closer to Hamersay; pass close to the fish cages to avoid reefs off Shealtragam. The best anchorage is northeast of Eilean Fear Vally; local boats have moorings there, but there is still space for visitors to anchor.

Approach from southeast, keeping 1½ cables off Hamersay to avoid McInnis Rock which dries 3·2 metres, heading for Sponish House, a conspicuous three-storey building, until east of Eilean Fear Vally, then turn west towards anchorage.

Sponish Harbour is cleaner than Charles Harbour, but the holding is poor.

Enter between Flodday, a large island on the northeast side of the loch, and Little Glas, less than a cable off its south side.

Ferramas On the west side of the pool between Flodday and Ferramas.

The best shelter is northeast of Ferramas, but drying reefs extend more than 1½ cables northwest from Flodday, and a submerged rock lies ½ cable east of the northeast point of Ferramas.

Loch Portain, the northeast arm of Loch Maddy, is well sheltered, especially east of the islet off the northeast shore but the bottom is soft mud in which some boats find it difficult to get an anchor to hold, and all sides are shoal.

Approach by the east side of Flodday; Mackay Rock ¾ cable from the east side of the channel dries 0·7 metre but it is well clear of the fairway. At the northeast point of Flodday the channel is a cable wide, but drying boulder banks reduce it to ⅓ cable, and the tide can be quite brisk.

The channel is again reduced to ¼ cable between the northeast shore and a small islet ½ mile further northwest, and a drying bank extends ½ cable west from Rubha nan Gall, the southeast point of Loch Portain, which lies ENE of the point.

A submerged rock spit extends more than ¾ cable south from the shore north of Rubha nan Gall, leaving a clear passage, less than ½ cable wide, south of it.

An islet in the middle of the loch 3 cables northeast of Rubha nan Gall is connected to the north shore by a drying reef; drying and submerged rocks lie 1 cable west of the islet.

Pass south of the islet and anchor not more than 2 cables beyond it, south of a small stone slip. The slip has been restored, and a post office with telephone and small shop are close by.

'Picnic anchorages' in suitable weather for a scramble ashore are:

Cable Bay (Bagh Chlann Neill), just inside the south point of the entrance, SE of Glas Eilean Mor. Acarsaid nam Madadh, SW of Glas Eilean Mor (very shoal) – avoid low spring tide.

Lighthouse beach northwest of Weaver's Point light beacon; Loch Scaaper close to shore is good for drinking, swimming, and catching trout.

Flodday, a bay on the east side of Flodday west of Mackay Rock. The inviting-looking inlet further south dries and is foul.

Passage notes between Skye and the Sound of Harris

Crossing the Little Minch from Skye to the Sound of Harris is straightforward in moderate weather. For Neist Point on the WSW of Skye see *The Yachtsman's Pilot to Skye and North West Scotland.*

Shelter on the west side of Skye may be found at Loch Dunvegan, Loch Snizort and, in some winds, Duntulm Bay.

Prawn creel buoys are scattered all over the Minch. International traffic uses the Minch, and a good lookout should be kept for commercial vessels.

Tidal streams in the Little Minch

Off Vaternish Point tidal streams run at a maximum of 2½ knots

The northeast-going stream begins –0350 Ullapool (+0415 Dover)

The south-going stream begins +0235 Ullapool (–0145 Dover)

Off the east coast of North Uist the tidal streams run at a maximum of 2 knots

The north-going stream begins –0550 Ullapool (+0215 Dover)

The south-going stream begins +0035 Ullapool (–0345 Dover)

Constant –0040 Ullapool (–0500 Dover)

Height in metres

MHWS	MHWN	MTL	MLWN	MLWS
4·6	3·5	2·6	1·9	0·6

Sound of Harris

Waypoint ¼ mile SSE of Fairway buoy 57°40'·1N 7°02'W

Caution

The Sound of Harris is a maze of rocks and islets and shallow passages; even the two principal passages through the sound should only be taken by yachts in settled moderate weather, using a large-scale chart and, even in light winds, a very heavy sea may be met at the northwest end of the sound.

Buoys have been laid for several passages (depending on the state of the tide and weather) across the Sound for a ferry service, and an edition of the chart which shows these buoys must be used.

Charts

2642 (1:20,000) is essential and must be corrected up to date. Hermetray anchorages could be approached using chart *1795* (1:100,000).

2841 (1:50,000), which also covers the west side of Harris, might be adequate for the main channels; a new edition which covers the whole of the Sound was published in 1996. OS map *18*.

Imray charts are available covering the West Coast of Scotland – Mallaig to Rudha Reidh and the Sound of Harris (*C66*) and North Minch and the Isle of Lewis (*C67*).

Tides

Tidal streams throughout the Sound of Harris are very variable not only between springs and neaps, but also between day and night and between summer and winter. The notes here should only be taken as a rough guide.

In the greater part of the Sound the flood runs eastward but, near the southwest shore, the flood runs inward from both ends towards Loch Mhic Phail and Loch Aulassary on North Uist.

In Caolas Skaari, which is about as central to the Sound as you can get, the SE-going (flood) stream begins +0545 Ullapool (+0125 Dover) and ends –0025 Ullapool (–0445 Dover). Generally the NW-going stream runs for the remainder of the time, but at neaps in summer the stream runs to the southeast during the day and to the northwest by night.

On the bar northeast of Berneray the tides turn about half an hour earlier.

Around the Hermetray group at the south point of the Sound, the NW-going (flood) stream begins –0535 Ullapool (+0230 Dover) and the SE-going tide begins +0035 Ullapool (–0345 Dover).

In narrow channels associated with Caolas Skaari the streams may reach 5 knots, and elsewhere 3 knots. In many places the streams may be diverted at right angles to the main channel by rocks and islets, and a constant watch must be kept to see that one is not being carried off course.

Dangers and marks (at the southeast entrance to the Sound of Harris)

Although there are many drying and submerged rocks further west, no concealed dangers extend more than ½ cable to seaward of any of the islands at the southeast end of the sound. The individual islands are not, however, easy to distinguish.

Cope Passage Fairway buoy (RW) 2¼ miles northeast of Crogary na Hoe, was repositioned in 2002.

Dun-aarin on the east side of the southeast approach to the Stanton Channel is conspicuously angular, and although much smaller in area than its neighbours is about the same height.

Crogary na Hoe, the northeast point of North Uist, is conspicuous.

Lights

Weaver's Point, Loch Maddy Fl.3s24m7M
Fairway buoy LFl.10s
Eilean Glas, Scalpay Fl(3)20s43m23M
Lt bns at Leverburgh (see page 76 below) may provide some guidance.

Anchorages and passages on the southwest side of the Sound

Waypoint ¼ mile S of Big Reef, Hermetray 57°38'·75N 7°02'·6W

Hermetray is the most southerly island in the Sound of Harris with Vaccasay on its west side. Several sheltered and easily accessible anchorages lie within a mile of Vaccasay. Tahay (64 metres), west of Vaccasay is the highest island of the group.

Tides

Tidal streams among the Hermetray Group run as follows:
The southeast-going stream begins about –0535 Ullapool (+0230 Dover)
The northwest-going stream begins +0035 Ullapool (+0345 Dover)
Streams in the narrower channels may reach 3 knots

Directions

From southeast drying reefs extend a cable south of Hermetray, and Angus Rock, a cable north of Groatay on the south side of the channel, dries 3 metres.

Pass midway between Hermetray and Groatay and, when the east end of Groatay is abeam, bring the summit of the Righe nam Ban group of islands ahead in line with Beinn Mhor 282° to pass north of Angus Rock as well as Mary Rock, over which the depth is charted as 2·1 metres, but tangle (weed) has been seen breaking the surface at a very low tide.

From northeast, identify Fairway buoy, then Greanem, ½ mile southwest of it. Greanem can be passed on either side but to the SSW, between Greanaem and Hermetray, there is a shoal area which, at low water and ebb tide with strong southeast winds, can be very choppy.

Pass midway between State Rock and Staffin Skerry which, in contrast to other rocks in the area, is sharp and angular.

To enter Vaccasay Basin, pass west of Staffin Skerry and midway between the skerry and Hulmetray – with care as reefs extend some way off either side.

Anchorages

Vaccasay Basin, from south pass west of Fuam, between Fuam and Vaccasay.

Dirt Rock, a cable east of Vaccasay, is charted as drying 3 metres, but reported in fact to show much less and fish cages are moored south of it.

Stanley Rock over which the depth is 1·8 metres lies a cable northeast of Fuam at the south end of the basin. Staffin Skerry in line with the southeast point of Scaravay, the most southeasterly island north of Cope Passage, bearing 039°, clears both these rocks.

Anchor in the northwest or southeast corners of the basin.

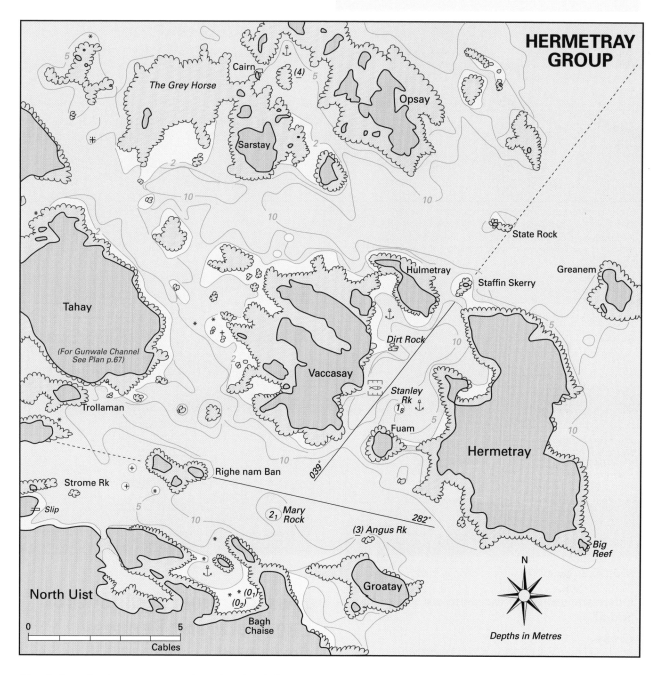

Shoal-draught boats can anchor in the inlet on Hermetray known as Acarsaid Mor, but this is shallow and rather constricted, with weed on the bottom, although the innermost part of the inlet is said to be free of weed. Water may be available from a spring near the east shore of Hermetray.

Bagh Chaise on North Uist lies southeast of Orasay, south of Righe nam Ban.

Drying reefs extend ½ cable east of Orasay; a detached rock which dries 1 metre lies just east of the middle of the entrance, and a reef extends more than ¼ cable ESE from Orasay.

Drying rocks lie more than ½ cable from the south shore. This bay is regarded as having the best shelter and best holding in the area.

Leading marks, consisting of a small white cairn above a white paint mark on the south shore 172°,

lead west of a rock west of the north end of Eileana Dubha and close east of a rock in the middle of the entrance. Do not stray to starboard of this line.

Orasay (Cheesebay), off a concrete slip on North Uist WNW of Orasay.

Approach by the south of Righe nam Ban, keeping closer to Orasay, and look out for Strome Rock which dries 2 metres, more than a cable northeast of the slip.

Opsay Basin (57°40'·5N 7°04'·3W), ¾ mile north of Vaccasay, is entered from southeast.

All sides of the basin are fringed by drying reefs and the only mark is the cairn on Grey Horse Island at the west side of the basin.

The best anchorage is northeast of a drying reef in the middle of the basin east of the cairn.

Bagh Chaise, North Uist, Sound of Harris, from E

Other anchorages at the southeast end of the Sound

Groay

(Waypoint ¼ mile S of Gilsay 57°42'·1N 7°00'W)

South of the entrance to Stanton Passage, provides some shelter on its north side. From the east this anchorage is best approached between Lingay and Gilsay. Northwest of Groay the buoys and perches for one of the new ferry routes mark channels to the north and west – but take care of tides.

Rodel, north of Renish Point on Harris, is described on page 77.

Passages from East towards Bays Loch and Berneray Causeway

Newton Ferry channel

This passage is part of one of the ferry routes between a terminal at Berneray Causeway and Leverburgh on Harris. It is intended for use by ferrymen who are thoroughly familiar with its features, and the marking has been amended several times during the last few years, so the chart must be correct up to date. From SE a yacht might approach this channel on various alternative unmarked courses from Cope Passage Fairway Buoy (which was itself repositioned in 2002).

Depending on visibility there is a choice of approaches to this channel. From Fairway Buoy, Sgeir a Chuain, 2m high, bears 322°. Steer to pass not more than a cable south of this rock keeping Sgeir an Iaruinn beacon just open north of Narstay

Hermetray Basin from WNW

light column to avoid a submerged rock further south, and continue on the same course to pass north of Narstay light column. Alter course to west to pass north of Bhrusda port-hand buoy ½M further west, and continue as described later below.

Alternatively, pass south of Cope Passage No.1 light buoy, and north of No.2 light buoy, and identify No.4 light buoy. About 1ca south of this buoy a skerry 0·6m high stands on a drying reef; halfway between No.2 and No.4 buoys steer west to pass 1ca south of the 0·6 skerry to pass between it and a detached reef, Sgeir a'Bhata Reothairt, another 1ca further south.

A further alternative is to continue along Cope Passage and pass between No.3 and No.4 buoys; identify Cabbage North light column and steer to keep it bearing not less than 270° to avoid an unmarked drying rock northeast of Cabbage South perch.

Whichever way you approach this passage, continue as follows:

Identify NF1 light column and steer to leave it 1ca to starboard, and then Narstay light column 1ca to port. Sgeir an Iaruinn unlit starboard-hand perch stands on a reef 3ca NW of Narstay light column, but note the reef extends south of a line between that perch and NF1.

Identify Bhrusda port-hand light buoy ½M west of Narstay and steer to pass north of it, and then north of NF2 port-hand light buoy and south of *NF5* starboard-hand light column. There are currently no buoys designated NF3 and NF4.

After passing NF5 continue west to NF6 port-hand light buoy, pass north of it and turn NNW to leave BA3 port-hand light column to port. Steer west to pass south of Trench starboard-hand light buoy, but note the drying rock charted 2 cables ESE of the buoy. Steer 280° towards the ferry slip breakwater at the north end of the causeway, pass north of Eilean Fuam and find suitable depth for anchoring in Loch nam Ban.

For Bays Loch leave Trench light buoy to port and steer NNW to pass northeast of McCaskill Rock light buoy, south of Drowning Rock light beacon and pass south and west of Catach west cardinal perch.

Note that there are depths of less than 1 metre in parts of this passage.

To make for the harbour, continue northwest, keeping a look out for reefs extending southeast and north of the breakwater, and pass round its head. Look out for traffic coming out. There is unlikely to be space for a yacht to berth in the harbour overnight.

To make for the north side of Bays Loch, identify the leading beacons close east of the school, bearing 025°, and steer on that course until within ½ cable of the shore, and then steer northwest to pick up a visitor's mooring or anchor as convenient.

Grey Horse Channel

Grey Horse Channel runs through an area of shoals and drying banks and rocks from Opsay Basin towards Bays Loch, Berneray and should only be considered by experienced rock-dodgers. The area is full of rocks with suggestive names, such as Drowning Rock, the Cabbage Patch, and Catach.

For the first 1¼ miles the passage is completely unmarked, after which some guidance will be found from buoys which mark the passage for the new ferry.

Grey Horse Channel should be taken on a rising tide with no swell, a light, preferably following, wind and the sun (if any) aft of the beam. The tide runs strongly across the passage and such marks as there are must be constantly watched to check that the yacht is not being carried sideways. The passage is easier if started at low water when at least some of the dangers are visible.

From Opsay Basin, pass north of the Grey Horse. A leading line for the next 1¼ miles is the highest point of Hermetray astern over the centre of the channel north of the Grey Horse 135°, but for the

Southeast end of Grey Horse Channel, looking southeast: Grey Horse Island on the right with the highest point of Hermetray beyond.

South side of the Sound of Harris looking NW along the line of the Grey Horse Passage. Opsay Basin is at right foreground and Berneray at top left

first cable keep south of this line to avoid a drying reef on the north side.

Sgeir a'Chruinn, which lies close south of the leading line 1¼ miles northwest of the Grey Horse, is just covered at half tide and shows white under water.

Identify NF2 light column and then NF5, and bring NF5 open north of NF2, bearing about 280° to avoid Sgeir a'Chruinn, and join Newton Ferry channel as above.

As one experienced yachtsman put it: 'A moment's lack of concentration could lead to unwanted problems.'

An alternative passage, between the east end of the Sound of Harris and the Sound of Berneray corresponding to one of the new buoyed ferry routes, is described on page 68.

Gunwale (or Rangas) Channel

This channel – best for boats without any underwater appendages – along the southwest side of the Sound lies outwith the limits of the current chart *2642*, but is included in earlier charts, although not with sufficient detail for navigation; the plan here is adapted from an edition of 1962. Ordnance Survey Explorer (1:25,000) map *454* (*NF87/97*) is some help.

For the benefit of those who cruise in open boats or small centreboarders, the following description is adapted from an account by the Brathay Exploration Group from Cumbria. Local fishermen use this passage, but not above half tide because the reefs are then covered. It would make an entertaining excursion in a dinghy. Note that the flood runs inward from both ends towards Loch Mhic Phail and Loch Aulassary and in places sets strongly across this channel.

Directions

From the southeast the passage begins between Tahay and Trollaman, where the width of the passage is further reduced by reefs on either side, but the least depth is 3 metres. After this, head for the north edge of Or Eilean about 292°, ¾ mile.

A couple of cables before the island, alter course to starboard heading for the peak of a peninsula on the southwest side of Votersay bearing 322°, to pass between the rock drying 2·0 metres and the reefs off Or Eilean. After passing the drying 2·0m rock, steer towards the summit of the right-hand part of Eilean na Gaoithe bearing 352°. For the reciprocal course, the east side of Or Eilean bears 172°.

When close to Eilean na Gaoithe identify Cleit nan Luch and alter course to port, and steer with the peak of that island in line with the south side of Eilean na Gaoithe astern 092°. This course leads among drying rocks and over a patch with a depth of 1 metre at chart datum to the beginning of the Rangas or Gunwale Channel which lies about 306° for about ¾ mile through a drying reef. At either

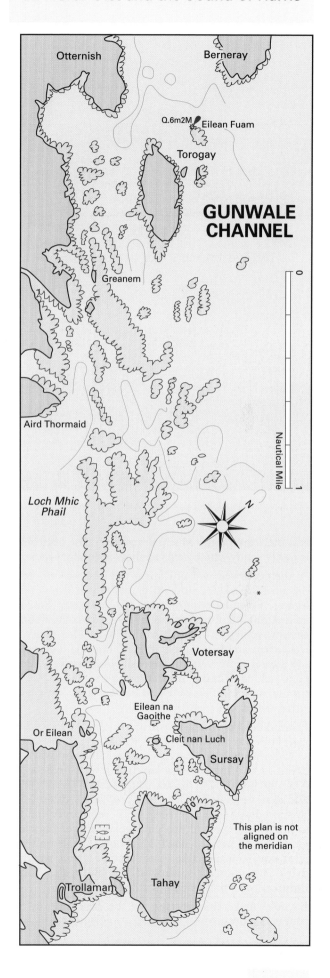

The narrow channel through Rangas Reef in the northern part of the Gunwale Channel

end there are points which almost dry. The botttom is partly sandy which helps to show individual rocks.

At the northwest end of Rangas the best water is on the northeast side, close to a reef which dries 3·5 metres. From here make good 301° towards Rubha na h-Aibhne Dubhe, making allowance for the flood stream setting in to Loch Mhic Phail. This course leads close south of a rock off Aird Thormaid drying 1·5 metres, which should be easily identified. When approaching Rangas from northwest the channel should be identified by the relatively high reefs on either side.

From Aird Thormaid a course of 310° towards the gap between Greanam and Rubha na h-Aibhne Dubhe passes over a patch south of Greanem with a depth of 0·7 metre. Pass southwest of a detached reef which dries 2·7 metres southwest of Greanem, and then head north close to a reef which dries 4·0 metres. Look out for reefs just submerged and drying to the west of this passage, and alter course gradually to port to head 322° beyond Otternish. This course leads close southwest of a reef which dries 2·5 metres southwest of Torogay, and northeast of a rock which just dries.

I would make this passage for the first time in a rubber dinghy.

Other channels

The new buoys provide opportunities for those whom a correspondent describes as 'Middle-League Rock-Hoppers'. The following directions should only be followed after plotting them on a chart which shows the marks, and identifying marks in place.

Note carefully the direction of buoyage in each channel.

Passage from east towards Bays Loch and Sound of Berneray

To continue through Sound of Berneray steer 280° to leave Trench buoy to starboard, taking care not to stray from the straight and narrow into shoal water on either side, and steer to pass north of En Fuam light beacon.

Lights
Reef Channel No.1 Q.G.2m4M
Reef Channel No.2 Iso.G.4s2m4M
Drowning Rock Q(2)G.8s2m2M
Harbour Iso.R.4s
Eilean Fuam Lt bn Q.6m2M
Berneray ferry slip 2F.G(vert)6m3M
Leac Bhan ferry slip 2F.R(vert)6m3M

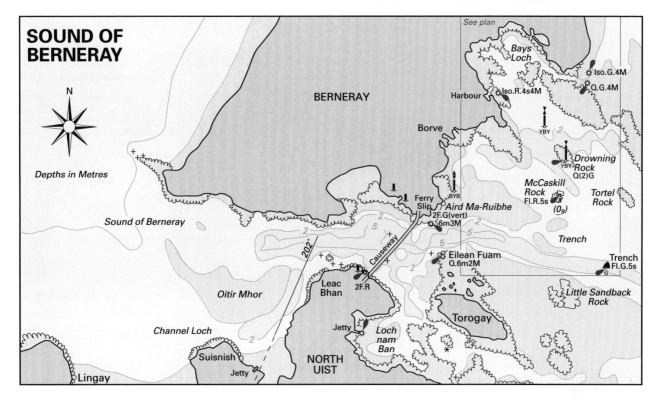

SOUND OF BERNERAY

Newton jetty root 2F.G(vert)9m4M
Cabbage North Lt col Fl.5s
NF1 Lt col Q(2)G.2s
Narstay Lt col Fl(2)R.8s
Bhrusda Lt buoy Fl.R.2s.
NF3 Lt buoy Fl.G.10s.
NF6 Lt buoy Fl.R.5s
BA3 Lt col Fl.(2)R.8s

Anchorage

Loch nam Ban, southwest of Eilean Fuam. Reefs dry one cable off either side of the entrance, and drying rocks lie in the middle of the loch.

Anchor in the mouth of the loch or, at neaps, further in, taking care to avoid the drying rocks. The bottom is soft mud so that a long keel yacht would sink in; care is needed to dig in anchor securely.

Bays Loch, Berneray

57°43'N 7°10'W

Tides in passage through The Reef

The southeast-going stream begins +0515 Ullapool (+0055 Dover)

The northwest-going stream begins –0125 Ullapool (–0545 Dover)

The stream runs at least 4 knots.

Constant –0046 Ullapool (–0506 Dover)

Height in metres

MHWS	MHWN	MTL	MLWN	MLWS
3·9	3·5	2·4	1·6	0·7

Directions

Pilotage around Berneray often involves rather ephemeral transits, along the lines of 'keep so-and-so's house *hidden*' which is hardly an appropriate direction to give to a stranger, but if taken in quiet weather, a step at a time, the pilotage can usually be puzzled out. Berneray is no place to make for in bad weather or poor visibility.

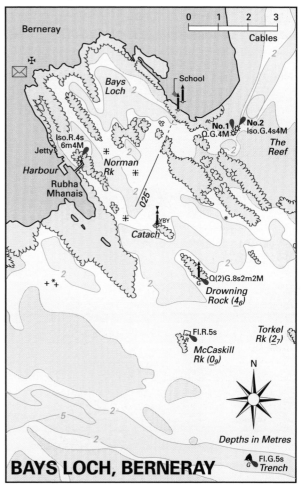

BAYS LOCH, BERNERAY

Loch nam Ban from SE

Berneray causeway from NW

Berneray, The Reef

Bays Loch, Berneray, from W. The Reef passage is at top left of centre, the harbour at bottom right

Passage through The Reef at Berneray, looking SW. The stream at the right gives some indication of the strength of the tide

For a brief daytime visit to Berneray in settled weather, approach by Cope Passage (see below), turn south from No.12 buoy and pass a cable from Massacamber, the northeast point of Berneray, between drying reefs off the point, and Cat Rocks which just dry, further off.

You can anchor off the sandy beach, but not too close to the beacons which mark the passage through the Reef, where the tide runs strongly, although the passage has been enlarged and should not prove too difficult. The channel has a depth of 1·5 metres below chart datum over a width of 35 metres.

To enter Bays Loch from the north pass close east of the two green light beacons and follow the deepest water round to starboard by eye, keeping about ½ cable off the shore, and anchor in the north corner of the bay which is sheltered except from southeast. A particularly careful lookout for rocks on either hand is needed here. A long mark for this leg of the course is Dunaarin, in line with the S beacon bearing 090° but, although Dunaarin is distinctive, it is more than 6 miles distant.

Two visitors moorings have been laid at the north side of the bay about a cable from the north shore.

Leading beacons on the NE shore, east of the school in line bearing about 025° lead through a channel across a spit extending west from The Reef. At the west end of the spit, a rocky patch just dries, and the line leads through the deepest water (probably awash at chart datum) just east of this patch. The line continues in clear water, west of Catach to the reef, part of which is above HW, west of the east cardinal perch off Ard Mhanish, the south point of Bays Loch. To make for the harbour, steer to pass 60m off the end of the breakwater.

Supplies

Shop at north side of the bay. Post office, telephone, Calor Gas at shop. Diesel and water at harbour.

Passage from south

To approach Bays Loch from south is impractical much below half tide.

Trench starboard-hand buoy is about ¾ mile NE of the ferry slip on Berneray; pass south of Trench buoy, steer NE for half a mile until Drowning Rock beacon is under Moor Hill at the north end of Berneray 351°, then steer on that bearing until 1 cable from Drowning Rock, and turn to port towards the harbour breakwater.

Then either steer to pass northeast of the breakwater and enter the harbour, or pick up the leading beacons to cross to the north side of Bays Loch. In either case a good lookout must be kept for the drying reefs and shoals.

Within two hours of HW in quiet weather one might just cross the banks NE of the ferry slip to pass southeast of new perch and east of BA4 light buoy.

Passages through the Sound of Harris

Cope Passage

Waypoint ¼ mile SSE of Fairway buoy 57°40'·1N 7°02'W

Waypoint at northwest entrance, a mile north of Berneray 57°45'·4N 7°10'W

The channel, which is marked principally for the use of shallow-draught army vessels, winds between drying rocks and is marked by light buoys. If these are passed on the correct hand in the right sequence it should present little problem as far as Berneray and can be used for a visit to that island.

Buoys in Cope Passage are of different sizes, which may cause confusion as to their relative distance.

Some years ago one of the buoys went missing, and was eventually found near Cape Wrath still flashing happily away; so don't take anything for granted. Additional buoys which have been laid for the ferry might be confusing to someone who didn't know they were there. For the approach to Bays Loch, see page 68.

At the northwest end of Cope Passage is a sand bar whose position varies, and which has been known to uncover. The channel is not marked at the bar, which would be dangerous in a westerly swell.

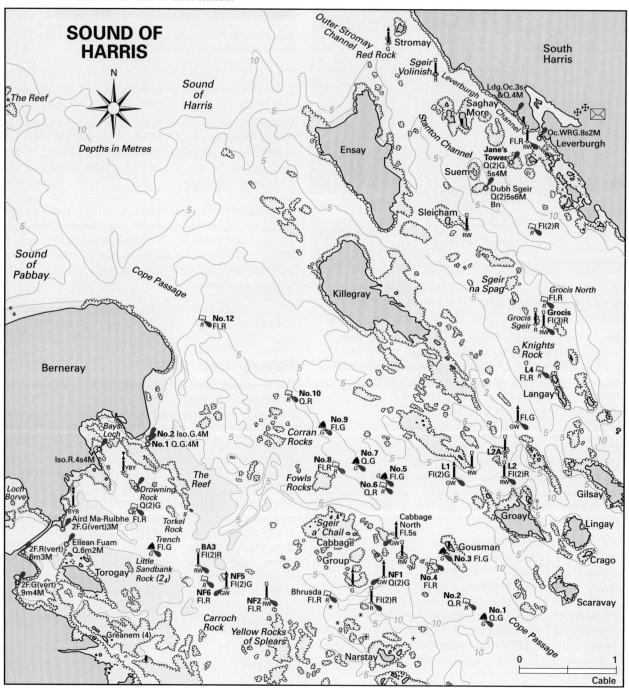

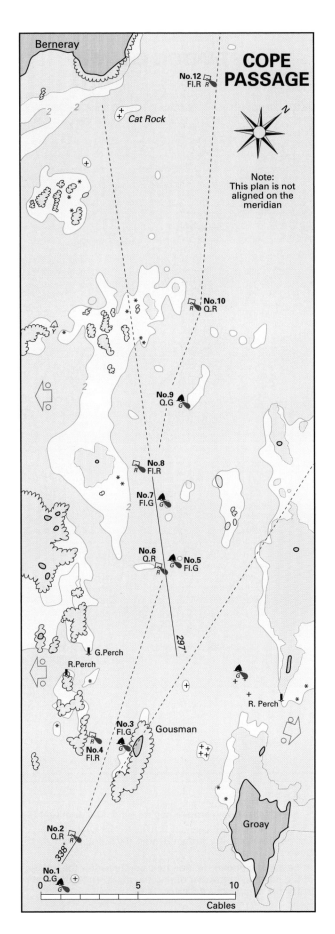

For a passage through the Sound of Harris, Stanton Channel, on the northeast side of the sound, is usually better.

Tides

At springs the southeast-going stream begins about +0515 Ullapool (+0055 Dover); the northwest-going stream begins –0125 Ullapool (–0545 Dover), but at neaps in summer the stream runs southeast during daytime for 8–9 hours.

Directions

Gousman, an islet 9 metres high, stands on an extensive drying reef near the southeast end of the passage, 1·7 miles NNW of Fairway buoy. From southeast steer with Gousman in line with a cairn on the summit of Killegray bearing about 338°.

Pass between light buoys No.1 to starboard and No.2 to port, then alter course to pass between light buoys No.3 and No.4. Continue on this course to pass between light buoys No.5 and No.6, watching the buoys astern to make sure you are not being carried off course.

Then steer with Moor Hill at the northeast end of Berneray bearing 297° to pass between light buoys No.7 and No.8. Alter course to starboard to leave light buoy No.9 to starboard and light buoy No.10 to port, and look for light buoy No.12, about a mile ahead under the north end of Pabbay.

Depths on the sand bar at the west end of the Cope Passage may vary and may not be as charted.

From northwest if any sea is running use Stanton Channel instead. In Cope Passage, if conditions are suitable at the bar approach with No.12 buoy in line with the north side of Groay as above. Pass north of No.10 buoy and south of No.9, and reverse the directions above.

Lights

The buoys are lit as shown on the plan, but there are no lights northwest of No.12. The passage is not recommended at night.

Stanton Channel

Waypoint ½ mile south of Renish Point 57°43'·5N 6°58'W

Waypoint at NW entrance, 1 mile south of Coppay 57°48'·7N 7°10'W

This is the main deep-water channel through the Sound of Harris, near the Harris shore; a safe passage depends on identifying and following a series of transits, sometimes at long range, although for a yacht the passage is less complicated than is shown on the Admiralty chart for larger craft.

Very heavy seas may be met at the northwest end of the passage, especially if an Atlantic swell is opposed by a northwest-going tide.

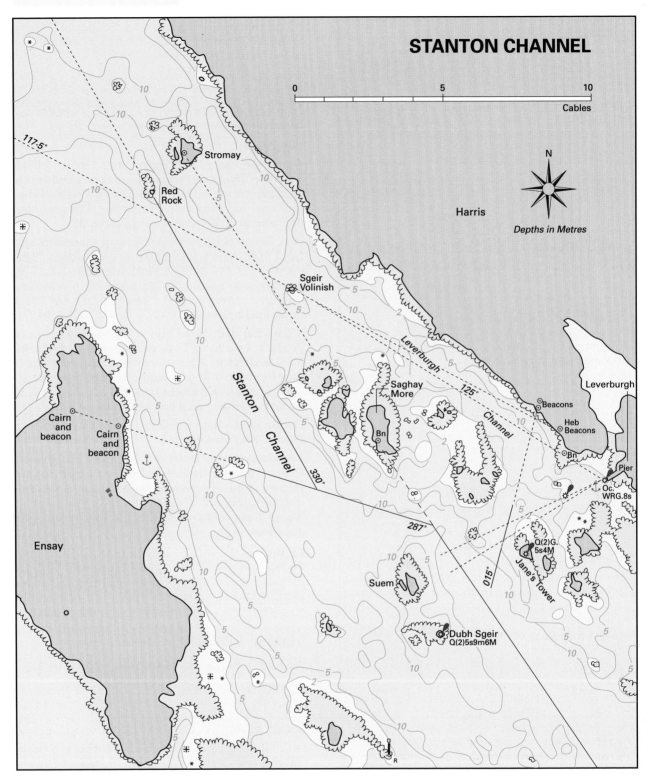

STANTON CHANNEL

0   5   10

Cables

N

Harris

Depths in Metres

Stromay

Red Rock

117.5°

Sgeir Volinish

Leverburgh

125°

Channel

Leverburgh

Beacons

Heb Beacons

Bn

Pier

Oc. WRG.8s

Cairn and beacon

Cairn and beacon

Stanton Channel

Saghay More

Bn

330°

287°

015°

Jane's Tower

Q(2)G. 5s4M

Ensay

Suem

Dubh Sgeir
Q(2)5s9m6M

R

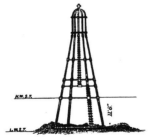

Red Rock Beacon

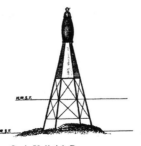

Sgeir Volinish Beacon

Tides

The southeast-going stream begins +0545 Ullapool (+0125 Dover)

The northwest-going stream begins –0025 Ullapool (–0445 Dover)

At neaps in summer the tide runs southeast for the whole of the day and northwest during the night. The spring rate is 4 knots southwest of Saghay More.

Approach to Sound of Harris from SE

Roneval

Approach to Sound of Harris from NW

Cape Difficulty — Coppay

Dangers and marks

The principal marks are:

Dun-aarin islet at the southeast end of the channel is prominently angular, 26 metres high.

Heb Beacon on Harris (a white tower, 16 metres high).

Jane's Tower on the northeast side of the channel (white at time of writing).

Dubh Sgeir beacon (red and black bands).

Other beacons are described in relation to each leading line, but there are many of them, and care is needed to be sure that the correct mark has been selected. The transits described must be carefully observed, especially if the course is against the tidal stream.

Directions

The southeast entrance is a mile wide between Renish Point and Dun-aarin, and the first three miles are straightforward. A course of 316° leads in the middle of the fairway to Stumbles Rock light buoy, ½ mile short of Dubh Sgeir. The islet of Suem close NNW of Dubh Sgeir in line with Coppay at the northwest end of Sound of Harris is on this bearing.

From the buoy, a stone beacon on Saghay More in line with a stone beacon on Stromay 325·5° lead clear of dangers between Dubh Sgeir and Jane's Tower; both beacons are similar in height so that the beacon on Stromay is hidden as Saghay More is approached.

After passing Suem, a pair of cairns and beacons on Ensay 287° in line leads clear of rocks southwest of Saghay More; the rear beacon is on top of the island, the front one black-and-white striped near the shore.

The next line consists of a conical green lattice beacon 10 metres in height on Red Rock which covers, 2 cables southwest of Stromay, in line with a beacon (alternatively if the beacon is not seen, the west end of a ruined chapel) bearing 330°, at Rubh'

an Teampuill a little inshore of Cape Difficulty, the southwest tangent of Harris.

The charted line for the northwest entrance to Stanton Channel is Sgeir Volinish beacon (9 metres high, red conical lattice) in line with Heb Beacon at Leverburgh 117½° and a yacht should not be south of this line for at least a mile northwest of Red Rock.

Alternatively bring Red Rock beacon in line with Sgeir Volinish beacon 122°.

If heading north after leaving Sound of Harris, Red Rock beacon in line with the summit of Saghay More astern 135° leads close south of Inner and Outer Temple Rocks off the Harris shore.

From northwest pass either side of Coppay and keep between ½ and 1 mile off the Harris shore until the marks are identified; Red Rock beacon should be seen first. The first danger is the drying rock Colasgeir, a mile north of Ensay. Select one of the transits above and pass 1 cable south of Red Rock.

Bring Red Rock astern in line with the beacon at Rubh' an Teampuill about 330°, then the beacons on Ensay in line 287°, followed by Saghay More stone beacon in line with Stromay stone beacon astern 325½°, which leads to Stumbles Rock buoy.

An alternative course close inshore is used by fishermen and there is often much less sea there; keep 1–2 cables off Rubh' an Teampuill to pass inshore of Inner and Outer Temple Rocks, then 1 cable off the 24-metre cliffs ¾ mile further southeast and through Sound of Stromay. Submerged rocks extend a cable north from the drying reef at the north end of Stromay.

Lights

Stumbles Rock Lt buoy Fl(2)R.10s
Dubh Sgeir bn Q(2)5s9m6M
Jane's Tower Q(2)G.5s6m4M
Leverburgh Reef Fl.R.2s
Leverburgh Pier head Oc.WRG.8s
Ldg bns W of Leverburgh 015° Q and Oc.3s

Leverburgh Channel

This channel, an alternative to the west part of Stanton Channel, is entered from south by passing a cable west of Jane's Tower with two light beacons on Harris in line about 015°.

When about a cable from the shore a small iron beacon SSE of Heb Beacon in line with Leverburgh pier head bearing 125° astern leads to the north of Sgeir Volinish.

From there pass south of Red Rock and continue as described above for Stanton Channel; alternatively take the Sound of Stromay, also described above.

Leverburgh

57°46'N 7°01·'5W

Tides

Constant –0040 Ullapool (–0500 Dover)

Height in metres

MHWS	MHWN	MTL	MLWN	MLWS
4·6	3·5	2·6	1·9	0·6

Dangers and marks

Drying reefs lie on the north side of Jane's Tower as well as between Fuam an t-Sruith and the head of the pier. A detached drying reef WSW of the pier is marked by a red and white light beacon.

Jane's Tower from south with Heb Beacon to the right and the two beacons for the Leverburgh Channel, with a white painted mark above them, to the left

Directions

Enter Leverburgh Channel as above and approach with the head of the pier open southeast of the R/W perch about 063°. Pass south of the perch and continue towards the pier; anchor as convenient clear of moorings. Leave space for ferry to manoeuvre.

Lights

At night the lights listed above (Leverburgh Channel) make the approach in darkness reasonably practicable.

Approach to Leverburgh, from W. Saghay More bottom left; Jane's Tower right, Heb Beacon, upper left of centre

Leverburgh

Supplies

Shop, tearoom/restaurant, post office, telephone, Calor Gas, diesel, petrol, water tap at pier.

Rodel

Waypoint ¼ mile east of Renish Point 57°43'·7N 6°57'·4W

Poll an Tigh-mhail is completely sheltered, but it is only accessible above half tide.

Chart
Included on *2642* (1:20,000); OS Explorer *455*

Tides
As Leverburgh.

Dangers and marks in Loch Rodel

Duncan Rock, ½ cable off the southwest shore, has a depth of 0·3 metres.

A submerged wreck lies in 12m towards the head of the loch, and a drying rock lies off the north side, west of a boulder beach.

Anchorage

Occasional anchorage can be found off the southwest shore, to wait for sufficient water to enter Poll an Tigh-mhail.

Poll an Tigh-mhail appears to have three entrances, but the middle one between the islands is much too obstructed by rocks ever to be considered. Sea Channel partly dries, with a stony bottom, and a boulder spit on the north side covers at half tide; it is dangerous in any swell.

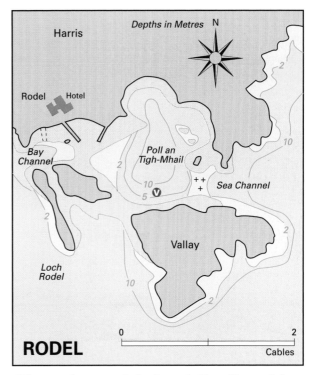

RODEL

The usual approach is through Bay Channel from Loch Rodel which dries 0·9 metre with coarse gravel and large stones on the bottom. Pillar Rock which covers, on the north side of the channel, is marked with a perch; when the base of the perch is covered the depth in the channel is 3·4 metres.

The pool itself is deep with a bottom of soft mud

77

Rodel

Services

The 18th-century Rodel Hotel was recently refurbished and now serves meals from 1200–1430 and 1730–2030 in both bars and restaurant. They also have shower and laundry facilities and internet access.

and there are many floats marking shellfish creels. Moorings for visitors have been laid on the north side of Vallay. The harbour on the north side of Bay Channel dries completely, but a yacht which is able to take the ground might dry out alongside one of its quays.

Rodel

IV. East coast of Harris

Crossing the Minch from Skye and the mainland

Crossing to the Hebrides from Gunna Sound, Sound of Mull, and from Canna to Barra and the Uists is described in Chapter I.

Crossing from Dunvegan or Uig presents no particular problem, nor, except for exposure, does a crossing from Gairloch or Loch Broom or the northern part of the mainland. Throughout the Minch the bottom is uneven and the sea may be very rough.

For details of the north of Skye see *The Yachtsman's Pilot to Skye and North West Scotland.*

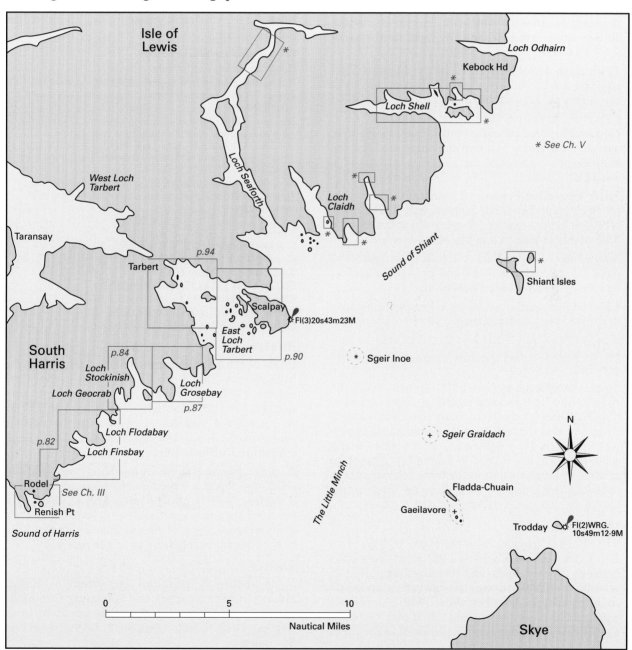

Charts

1794 or *1795* (1:100,000). *2210* (1:50,000) shows the north end of Skye in greater detail. OS map *14*.

Tides

Off Rubha Hunish the northeast-going stream begins –0405 Ullapool (+0400 Dover).

The southwest-going stream begins +0220 Ullapool (–0200 Dover).

Off Scalpay, Harris, the northeast-going stream begins –0305 Ullapool (+0500 Dover) at springs and –0505 Ullapool (+0300 Dover) at neaps, beginning at NNE and gradually turning to east.

The southwest-going stream begins +0320 Ullapool (–0100 Dover) at both springs and neaps. This has the effect that at neaps the NNE-going tide runs for 8½ hours and the southwest-going tide for 4 hours.

Northeast-going streams run at 2½ knots at springs, but both streams vary according to the wind direction and strength.

Dangers and marks (described in sequence from Skye towards Harris)

A group of islets of which the largest is Fladda-chuain lies between 2½ and 3½ miles northwest of Rubha Hunish.

Sgeir nam Maol beacon, 12 metres high, with six legs and a cylindrical cage with a cross on top, is at the centre of a patch of rocks 2½ miles NNW of Rubha Hunish.

Comet Rock red can light buoy is more than a mile east of these rocks. (One of the ships used for the hydrographic surveys of the Hebrides in the 1850s was HMS *Comet*.)

Sgeir Graidach beacon, of a similar shape to that on Sgeir nam Maol but painted red, is 2¾ miles NNW of Fladda-chuain. Eugenie Rock lies ½ mile SSE of this beacon at a depth of 0·9 metre.

Sgeir Inoe, 3 miles ESE of Eilean Glas lighthouse dries 2·3 metres, and is marked by a green conical light buoy nearly a mile NNW of it.

Eilean Glas lighthouse on the east point of Scalpay is a white tower with red bands, 30 metres in height.

The bottom of the Little Minch is very uneven, and strong wind and tide together with any swell create very heavy seas.

Large commercial vessels pass through the Little Minch and are recommended to pass between Troddday and Comet Rock buoy in a northeasterly direction, and through Sound of Shiant and northwest of Sgeir Inoe light buoy in a southwesterly direction, but this is not a mandatory separation scheme. A good lookout needs to be kept for vessels following these tracks – as well as for those which ignore the recommendations.

Directions

The shortest crossing from the north of Skye is to East Loch Tarbert, Harris and the direct line passes between Comet Rock and Fladda-chuain, but it may be preferable to keep downwind or downtide from the dangers described above. With a southwest wind and/or a northeast-going tide it may be better to pass east of Troddday and northeast of all the rocks

and enter East Loch Tarbert by Sound of Scalpay.

On a passage to the Sound of Harris from north Skye there are no hidden dangers. An t-Iasgair, 21 metres high, lies about 3 miles WSW of Rubha Hunish.

A course from north Skye to the north part of Lewis passes close to the Shiant Islands which lie between 10 and 12 miles north of Rubha Hunish. If making for Loch Shell heavy seas in the Sound of Shiant are avoided by passing east of the Shiant Islands. The east end of Eilean Mhuire, the most easterly island, is clean, but rocks above water and drying extend 1¼ miles west of Garbh Eilean, the most westerly island; for details of the Shiants see page 102.

For the passage north of Gob na Milaid see page 105.

From Gairloch or Loch Broom the shortest crossing is to Tob Limervay in Loch Shell; a passage to East Loch Tarbert, Harris, passes close south of the Shiant Islands.

Tides around the Shiant Islands

Tides run strongly as follows:

The north-going stream begins –0320 Ullapool (+0445 Dover). The south-going stream begins +0305 Ullapool (–0115 Dover).

The spring rate of the south-going stream is 2 knots, but the streams bend south of the Shiant Islands to run WSW and ENE. 1 mile southeast of the islands the rate in both directions is 3 knots with heavy overfalls during the east-going stream.

Around Shiant South Rock, 2½ miles southwest of the Shiant Islands, the streams are rotatory but follow the same pattern.

Lights

Eilean Troddday Fl(2)WRG.10s52m12-9M
Comet Rock Lt buoy Fl.R.6s
Sgeir Inoe Lt buoy Fl.G.6s
Eilean Glas LtHo Fl(3)20s43m23M
Shiants Lt buoy Fl.G
Rubh' Uisenis Lt bn Fl.5s24m11M
Gob na Milaid Lt bn Fl.15s17m10M

At night

Look out for large commercial vessels. Crossing from Skye to East Loch Tarbert keep in the white sector of Eilean Troddday light beacon and pass northeast of Sgeir Inoe light buoy; Sound of Scalpay is easier for a stranger at night than the passage south of Scalpay, but approaching East Loch Tarbert in the dark is best avoided altogether.

A night passage to or from Stornoway without electronic devices depends on bearings of Eilean Troddday, Gob na Milaid and Arnish Point light beacons, but their nominal range is such that at their furthest range, east of Shiant Islands, each would only be faintly visible for part of the passage.

Shelter

Some shelter in Duntulm Bay south of Rubha Hunish (northwest Skye), and Kilmaluag Bay on the east side of Skye. Good shelter in East Loch Tarbert, Loch Claidh, Loch Shell, Loch Erisort and Stornoway.

Coastal passage from Renish Point to East Loch Tarbert

The coast is very deeply indented, with few features to assist identification and several dangerous rocks up to 2 cables from the shore, although none affect a direct passage from Renish Point to East Loch Tarbert outwith this distance from the shore.

Chart

1795 (1:100,000). There are no larger-scale charts, and the plans in this book are based on Admiralty surveys from about 1860 at a scale of 1:10,560, supplemented by individual observations. OS Explorer *455* is strongly recommended owing to the small scale of the chart.

Tides

(Interpolated between Leverburgh and Tarbert)
Constant −0035 Ullapool (−0455 Dover)
Height in metres

MHWS	MHWN	MTL	MLWN	MLWS
4·8	3·8	2·8	2·0	0·7

Dangers and marks

Roneval (Roinebhal), behind Rodel, is 458 metres high but further northeast the hills stand back from the coast and are not so high. A lattice radio mast stands about a mile north of Rodel.

Rubha Quidnish, 4 miles from Renish Point, has the appearance of being split into blocks; drying rocks lie 1½ cables outside the islands southwest of Rubha Quidnish.

Ard Manish (Aird Mhanais), on which a small triangulation pillar stands, has drying rocks up to 1½ cables south and east of it.

Rubha Cluer (Chluar), 3 miles northeast of Rubha Quidnish, is steep-sided with a grassy top and a small stone cairn on its summit. A rock which dries 2·9 metres lies a cable southeast of the point.

Lights

There are none southwest of the entrance to East Loch Tarbert, but the following will be of some help:
Eilean Glas, Scalpay, East Loch Tarbert
  Fl(3)20s43m 23M
Neist Point, Skye Fl.5s43m16M
Waternish Point, Skye Fl.20s21m8M
Rodel is included in Chapter III as it appears on the chart of the Sound of Harris.

Anchorages

Lingarabay, 57°45'N 6°56'W, provides some shelter in westerly winds, but the west end of the inlet is too much obstructed by rocks for a yacht to go much further in than abreast of Eilean Collam and there is a loading jetty for a quarry in the inlet (this is the site of one of several proposed 'superquarries'). Submerged rocks lie more than a cable from the shore, 4 cables east of the entrance.

Loch Finsbay

Waypoint ¼ mile east of Finsbay Island 57°46'·N 6°53'·5W

The entrance lies ¾ mile southwest of Rubha Quidnish, between Finsbay Island, which is 17 metres high, steep-sided with grass on top, on the south side, and Eilean Quidnish which is 13 metres high with a sharper peak.

Drying and submerged rocks lie up to a cable north of Finsbay Island, and drying reefs and submerged rocks lie up to 2 cables ESE and northeast of Eilean Quidnish.

Directions

From south, do not turn into the loch until about midway between the two islands.

From northeast keep Ard Manish open east of Rubha Quidnish 032° astern to clear the rocks east of Eilean Quidnish.

Inside the loch, keep Eilean Druim an Tolla, which is at the tip of a promontory on the south side, bearing 290° to avoid drying rocks on the north side of the channel, then pass a cable north of Eilean Druim an Tolla.

Turn to starboard and steer with the promontory off which Eilean Druim an Tolla lies bearing 194° astern, and the conspicuous bluff on the east side of an inlet ahead bearing 014° (not the inlet further east), passing about ¾ cable east of Ardvey, between Sgeir na h-Acarsaid which dries 1·5 metres and drying reefs off Ardvey. Fish cages occupy part of the anchorage.

Anchorages

Ardvey Anchor north of Ardvey in 4 metres, rather soft mud. Post office, telephone and small shop west of Ardvey. Some private moorings.

Loch Flodabay, 57°47'N 6°52'W, is not particularly recommended, but the original Admiralty survey shows a passage about ¾ cable wide northeast of several drying and submerged rocks all lying 1 cable from the northeast shore.

Loch Geocrab and Loch Beacravik

Waypoint ¼ mile east of Earr Manish 57°46'·3N 6°50'·3W

Ard Manish, described above, has detached drying rocks off its south and east sides.

Allister Rock which dries 1·7 metres lies 1½ cables south of the point, and Earr Manish which dries 2·3 metres lies more than 2 cables east of the point.

A large shed (salmon hatchery), with a stone gable facing seaward and red sides, stands at the head of Loch Beacravik. This building kept in sight at the west side of the entrance, about 330°, leads east of Earr Manish, off Ard Manish.

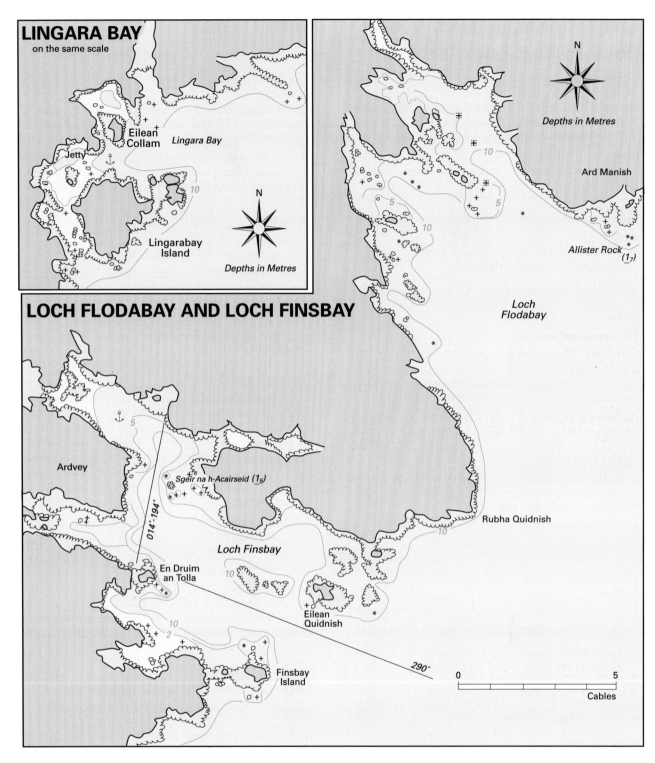

LINGARA BAY
on the same scale

Eilean Collam

Lingara Bay

Jetty

Lingarabay Island

N

Depths in Metres

N

Depths in Metres

Ard Manish

Allister Rock (1₇)

Loch Flodabay

LOCH FLODABAY AND LOCH FINSBAY

Ardvey

Sgeir na h-Acairseid (1₅)

014°-194°

Rubha Quidnish

Loch Finsbay

En Druim an Tolla

Eilean Quidnish

290°

Finsbay Island

0   5
Cables

Directions

From north head for Ard Manish then Eilean Mhanais and when the salmon hatchery has been identified approach it bearing 330° as above to clear rocks south and west of Aird Mhor. Sgeir Dubh, an above-water rock off the southwest point of Stockinish Island in line with the HW line of the tidal islet at the southeast point of Stockinish Island 073° leads close south of a rock which dries 3·0 metres, south of the southern entrance to Loch Stockinish.

In the entrance to Loch Beacravik rocks dry more than half of its width from the east side; keep a quarter of the width from the west side.

Within the loch there are shoal rocky patches which give poor holding so that the anchor needs to be placed with care. Some fish cages are laid on the east side of the loch.

Loch Geocrab provides little shelter, apart from a pool at the head of the loch behind a drying reef, and is also obstructed by fish cages.

Loch Beacravik and Geocrab

Loch Beacravik from northwest. The salmon hatchery is left of centre

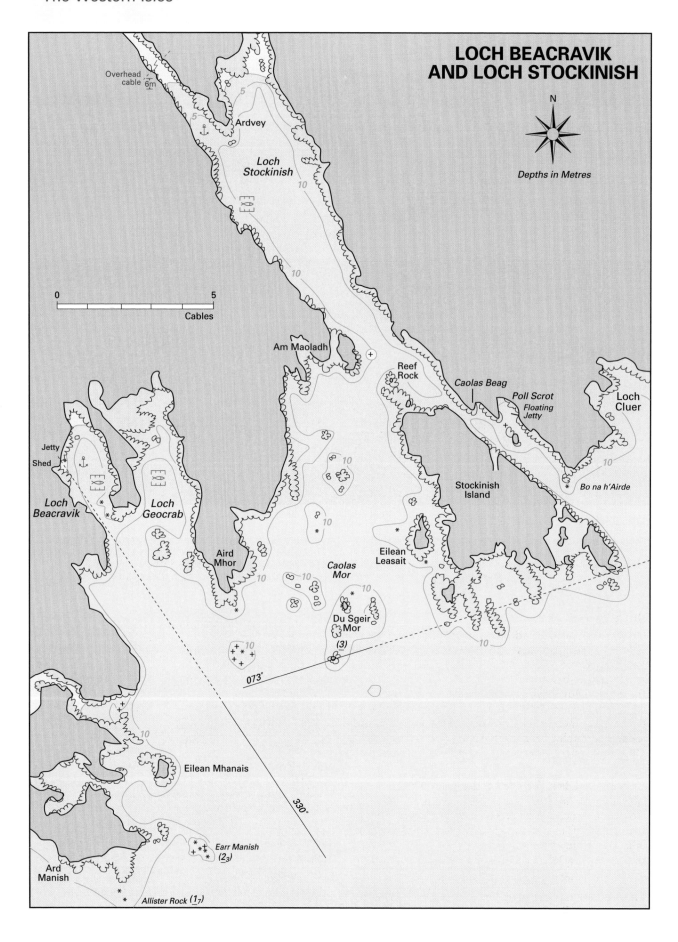

LOCH BEACRAVIK
AND LOCH STOCKINISH

N

Depths in Metres

Overhead
cable 6m

Ardvey

*Loch
Stockinish*

5

5

10

10

0   5

Cables

Am Maoladh

Reef
Rock

Caolas Beag

Poll Scrot
*Floating
Jetty*

Loch
Cluer

Jetty

Shed

*Loch
Beacravik*

*Loch
Geocrab*

Aird
Mhor

10

10

10

Stockinish
Island

Bo na h'Airde

10

Eilean
Leasait

*Caolas
Mor*

10

10

10

Du Sgeir
Mor

(3)

10

073°

10

330°

Eilean Mhanais

10

Earr Manish
(2₃)

Ard
Manish

Allister Rock (1₇)

Loch Beacravik entrance from northwest, showing how far the rocks extend from the east side

Loch Stockinish

Waypoint ¼ mile south of Rubha Chluar 57°48'·1N
6°47'·4W (for waypoint for Caolas Mor see Loch Gheocrab)

Dangers and marks

Caolas Mor, the broader entrance to the loch, west of Stockinish Island, is littered with rocks, most of which cover and Caolas Beag, described below, is more straightforward.

Du Sgeir Mor stands above water on a reef in the middle of the entrance and a rock which dries about 1 metre lies nearly a cable southeast of it. A clean passage 2 cables wide lies between this rock and islets and drying rocks off the west side of Stockinish Island.

A drying rock lies ¾ cable off the west side of Eilean Leasait, the largest island off the west side of Stockinish Island. A rock which dries 2 metres lies a little west of mid-channel 3 cables northwest of Eilean Leasait.

These are not the only rocks in Caolas Mor, but they are the ones which affect the fairway.

The main part of Loch Stockinish is entered between Reef Rock which rarely covers, more than a cable northwest of Stockinish Island and Am Maoladh, a tidal islet on the northwest side of the passage.

A submerged rock known as Bo of the Den lies at a depth of 1·8 metres nearly a cable east of Am Maoladh.

Approach midway between Du Sgeir Mor and Eilean Leasait heading NNW; when the north end of Eilean Leasait is abeam steer towards the north end of Stockinish Island for about ¼ mile, then NNW towards the west side of Am Maoladh and pass midway between Reef Rock and Am Maoladh.

Caolas Beag, on the northeast side of Stockinish Island, is less than 30 metres wide at one point but apart from Bo na h' Airde which covers at about half tide on the east side of the entrance, it is clean.

A rock above water stands on a reef off the mouth of Poll Scrot on the north side of the channel with submerged rocks between the rock and the promontory northwest of it.

The northeast side of the narrowest part of the channel dries off, leaving a channel 27 metres wide.

Poll Scrot A concrete quay with timber facing, and a floating jetty, lie on the east side and several inshore fishing boats lie at moorings there.

Services

Water, diesel, 13A electricity, toilet, 1-ton crane.

Caolas Beag, Stockinish, from SSE. Stockinish Island at left

Poll Scrot

Inner part of Loch Stockinish

Rocks north and northwest of Stockinish Island have already been described; drying rocks extend up to ½ cable from the northeast shore opposite Reef Rock; to avoid Bo of the Den keep northeast of mid-channel.

There are fish cages in the main part of the loch. Drying rocks extend ¾ cable SSE from Ardvey, the promontory dividing the two arms of the head of the loch; anchor in the mouth of the northwest arm. The only facility is a post office halfway along the east side of the loch.

Overhead power cables with a safe clearance of not more than 6 metres cross the northwest arm about 2 cables from its entrance

A rock which dries 2·9 metres, 1 cable southeast of Rubha Cluer is not shown on older copies of chart *1795*.

Loch Grosebay

Waypoint about ½ mile ESE of Cairam 57°49′N 6°58′W

This loch has several islets and drying rocks in it and the shelter at the head is not good, but a very small inlet on the north side, Loch Scadabay, gives excellent shelter.

Cairam, an islet 22 metres high stands in the middle of the entrance and Glas Sgeir stands on a drying reef a cable north of Cairam.

Sgeir na h'Iolla dries nearly a cable off the northeast shore, southeast of the entrance to Loch Scadabay. Rubha Reibinish open south of Aird Bheag 083° leads south of Sgeir na h'Iolla.

Patrick's Bo, which dries 1·5 metres, lies about 3 cables NNW of Glas Sgeir; the northeast sides of both Glas Sgeir and Cairam in line 153° astern lead close east of Patrick's Bo.

John Rock which dries 3 metres lies ¼ mile NNW of Patrick's Bo near the northeast shore, and a rock

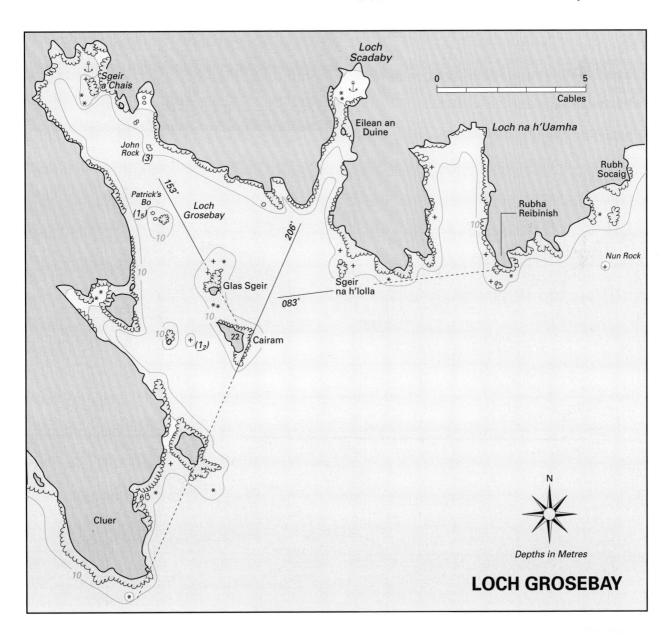

LOCH GROSEBAY

Depths in Metres

which dries 1·5 metres lies ½ cable south of Sgeir a' Chais, which is marked by a cairn near the head of the loch.

Directions

From southwest the drying rock off Rubha Cluer described above must be avoided, and from the east Nun Rock, which is described below, is a hazard. For the head of the loch pass northeast of Patrick's Bo and then keep to the southwest side of the loch and anchor north of Sgeir a' Chais.

Loch Scadabay may be found, if it is not otherwise apparent, by lining up the west side of Cairam with Rubha Cluer 206°. The passage west of Eilean an Duine is only 30 metres wide; after passing the island keep to starboard to avoid a rock-fall at the base of a cliff on the west side.

A rough concrete jetty stands on the east side of the channel, and the head of the loch opens up to a basin with a depth of less than 2 metres of very soft mud in which a yacht's keel will come to no harm. Drying rocks in the middle of the entrance to this pool can be avoided by keeping to the southeast side.

Nun Rock lies 2 cables offshore at a depth of 0·6 metres, ¼ mile south of Rubha Bocaig at the south entrance to East Loch Tarbert. There is no clearing mark for the south side of Nun Rock.

Loch Scadabay

Loch Scadabay from its head; the rocks in the middle of the pool are not quite covered

East Loch Tarbert

Waypoint 1 cable south of Sgeir Griadach light buoy
57°50'·3N 6°41'·3W

A broad loch with many bays providing a choice of anchorages. Braigh Mor, the main fairway, has various rocks and islets on either side.

Scalpay, a substantial island 2½ miles long, lies on the north side of the entrance, separated from Harris by the Sound of Scalpay, which is only a cable wide at one point. Sound of Scalpay is much the most straightforward approach, particularly from east or northeast. A bridge across the Sound of Scalpay has a headroom of 20 metres.

Scotasay stands in the middle of the loch, 8 cables west of Scalpay, and Tarbert village and ferry terminal are 2 miles further northwest.

Chart

2905 (1:10,000). OS Explorer *455*

Tides

The northwest-going stream in Braigh Mor flows round Scalpay to run east in Sound of Scalpay and begins –0520 Ullapool (+0245 Dover). The southeast-going stream (west-going in Sound of Scalpay) begins +0105 Ullapool (–0315 Dover).

Constant –0026 Ullapool (–0446 Dover)

Height in metres

MHWS	MHWN	MTL	MLWN	MLWS
5·0	3·7	2·9	2·1	0·8

Dangers and marks (in Braigh Mor)

Eilean Glas lighthouse at the most easterly point of Scalpay is a white tower with red bands, 30 metres in height.

Skerries and islets, of which the main group is the Gloraigs, extend up to 7 cables from the southwest shore of the loch. The most northeasterly of the Gloraigs is Dun Corr Mor on which is an inconspicuous light beacon.

When approaching from south, Nun Rock, described above, is just cleared on its east side by keeping Eilean na Sgaite, 8 cables south of Dun Corr Mor, open of Sgeir Bhocaig, a rock 3 metres high close to Rubha Bhocaig, the southwest point of the entrance, bearing 008°.

Bogha Bhocaig, over which the depth is 1·4 metres, lies 4 cables east of Rubha Bhocaig and may be dangerous in a swell. Dun Corr Mor, the most northeasterly of the Gloraigs, under the summit of Scotasay 342° leads 2 cables east of Bogha Bhocaig. Sgeir an Leum Bhig, the most southeasterly of the Gloraigs, touching Stiughay, east of Scalpay 004°, leads clear west of Bogha Bhocaig.

In the approach from east, Bogha Lag na Laire, a group of rocks which just dries, lies 3 cables south of Meall Chalibost, the southern extremity of Scalpay.

Sgeir Griadach, a patch of rocks, part of which dries 1·5 metres, 4 cables south of Scalpay, is marked on its south side by a south cardinal light buoy (note that this is nothing to do with Sgeir Graidach, a few miles east in the middle of the Minch).

Approaching from east or northeast, Sgeir Griadach light buoy must be identified and approached on a bearing of not less than 260°; keep outwith the 40-metre contour until south of this line.

South harbour, Scalpay

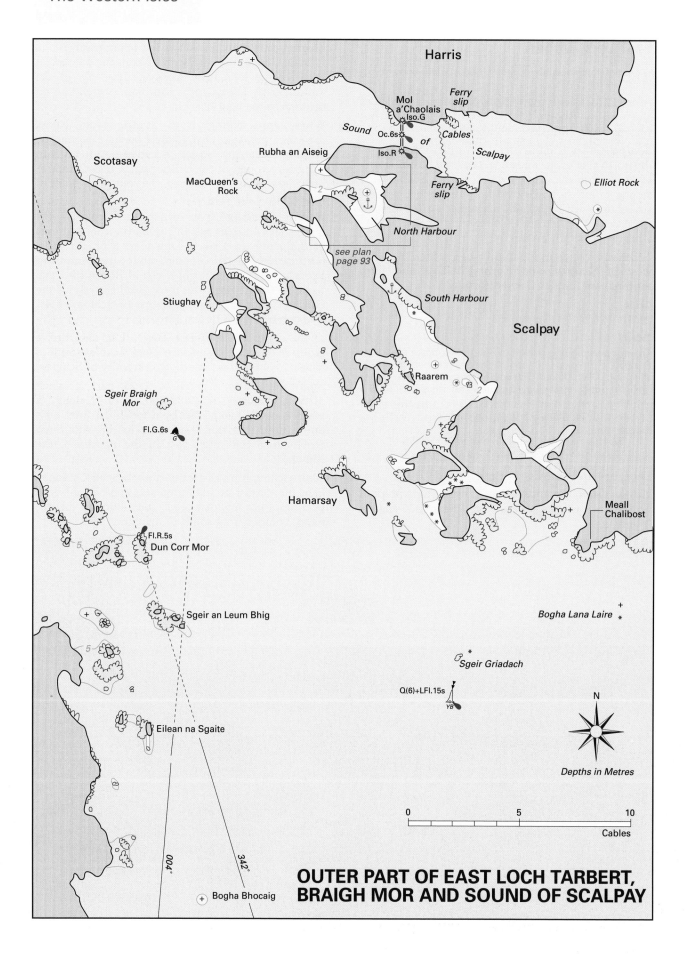

Harris

Mol
a'Chaolais   *Iso.G

Oc.6s

Sound   *Iso.R*

Rubha an Aiseig

Ferry
slip

Cables

of

Scalpay

Ferry
slip

Elliot Rock

Scotasay

MacQueen's
Rock

North Harbour

2

South Harbour

Stiughay

Scalpay

Sgeir Braigh
Mor

Raarem

2

Fl.G.6s
G

5

Fl.R.5s
Dun Corr Mor

Hamarsay

Meall
Chalibost

5

5

Sgeir an Leum Bhig

5

Bogha Lana Laire

Sgeir Griadach

Q(6)+LFl.15s
YB

N

Eilean na Sgaite

Depths in Metres

004°

342°

0   5   10
Cables

**OUTER PART OF EAST LOCH TARBERT,
BRAIGH MOR AND SOUND OF SCALPAY**

Bogha Bhocaig

see plan
page 93

Sgeir Braigh Mor, 6 cables north of Dun Corr Mor, is marked on its south side by a green conical light buoy.

Bogha Ruadh, on the southwest side of the fairway a mile northwest of Dun Corr Mor, dries 0·5 metre. A pair of islands, Eileanan a' Ghille-bheid, lies ½ mile beyond Bogha Ruadh and a further ½ mile northwest is a larger island, Eilean Arderanish. Eilean Arderanish open northwest of Eileanan a' Ghille-bheid 305° clears the northeast side of Bogha Ruadh.

A light beacon 5 metres high stands on Sgeir Ghlas, on the southwest side of Scotasay.

Lights

Eilean Glas lighthouse Fl(3)20s43m23M
Sgeir Griadach Lt buoy Q(6)+LFl.15s
Dun Corr Mor Lt beacon Fl.R.5s10m5M
Sgeir Braigh Mor Lt buoy Fl.G.6s
Sgeir Ghlas Lt bn Iso.WRG.4s9m9-6M
Tarbert pier and dolphin each 2F.G(vert)5M

At night

From south keep at least a mile offshore (Eilean Glas bearing not more than 048°) until Dun Corr Mor light is in line with Sgeir Ghlas light and turn to head to the east of Sgeir Braigh Mor light buoy until in the white sector of Sgeir Ghlas light.

From east or northeast, Sound of Scalpay is the more straightforward approach. North Harbour, Scalpay has a light Fl.G on the buoy northeast of Coddem as well as 2F.G(vert) at the seaward end of the pier, and may be approached by way of Sound of Scalpay if there is less than total darkness.

If approaching by Braigh Mor, the south passage, Sgeir Griadach light buoy must be identified and approached on a bearing of not less than 260°; keep outwith the 40-metre contour until south of this line.

Keep in the white sector of Sgeir Ghlas light beacon passing Dun Corr Mor light beacon to port, and Sgeir Braigh Mor light buoy to starboard. Pass south and west of Sgeir Ghlas light beacon until in its northwest white sector, and steer with that light astern to Tarbert.

Sound of Scalpay

Waypoint about ½ mile ESE of Rubha Craigo 57°52'·6N 6°39'W

A clean but narrow passage north of Scalpay. Drying rocks extend up to a cable off the northeast shore of Scalpay outwith the entrance. Elliot Rock, at a depth of 2 metres, lies 1½ cables off the head of a bay on the south side of the channel.

A reef which extends more than ½ cable southeast of Mol a' Chaolais, at the west side of the bay at the north ferry slipway dries 1·4 metres (so don't tack close inshore there).

The bridge across the sound has a headroom of 20 metres.

Lights

Bridge Oc.6s and Iso.G and Iso.R

Plocrapool from south with the Gloraigs and Scotasay beyond

Plocrapool

Anchorages in the outer loch

Plocrapool, 57°50'·5N 6°45'W, is a snug but shallow anchorage on the southwest side of the entrance to Braigh Mor. Approach by south of Dun Corr Mor and pass northwest of Sgeir Bun a' Loch which is in the middle of the entrance, closer to that rock than to the islands on the west side to avoid drying reefs off them. At spring tides look out for rocks at a depth of less than 2 metres although these are not likely to be a problem at other times. Head to the east of houses steering 210° and anchor as far in as the depth allows (see plan of inner loch).

South Harbour, Scalpay, 57°52'N 6°42'W. Identify Hamarsay and Rossay (the highest of the islands southwest of Scalpay), and pass between them and midway between Raarem and the southeast shore to avoid drying rocks SSE of Raarem. When Raarem is abaft the beam and the promontory on the west shore is well open north of Raarem turn to pass ½ cable from its east side to clear Boundary Rock over which the depth is 0·4 metre and then keep close to the west side at the narrows. Anchor southeast of the islet off the southwest side of the inner loch, clear of a drying rock 50 metres from the shore ½ cable southeast of the islet. There is deep water further in, but more rocks than water, and several moorings.

At Eilean Glas there is a very occasional anchorage in an inlet ¾ cable west of the lighthouse. A rock which dries 1 metre lies ½ cable south of the east point of the entrance and an overhead cable with a clearance of 9 metres crosses the head of the inlet from a point just north of the jetty on the east side.

South Harbour, Scalpay, from the head of the inlet

North Harbour, Scalpay

57°52'·5N 6°42'W

Dangers and marks

MacQueen's Rock, 1½ cables west of Rubha na Cudaigean at the south side of the entrance, covers at high water.

Rocks extend ⅓ cable west of Rubha an Aiseig on the north side of the entrance and a rocky shelf lies on the north side of the entrance channel.

A drying wreck lies on the south side of the channel, northwest of Coddem, and a green conical light buoy lies northeast of Coddem.

A submerged rock at a depth of 1·1 metres is charted north of the middle of the harbour; an attempt was made to remove it with explosives but there is some doubt as to whether this was successful.

The stranded hulk of a ferrocement coaster from World War I lies in the northeast corner and fishing boats lie on its north side overnight.

Directions

Give Rubha an Aiseig a berth of at least ½ cable and keep in mid-channel in the entrance; pass north of the light buoy and anchor clear of the fairway to the pier, which is frequently used. Landing is most convenient at a slip ¼ cable east of the pier.

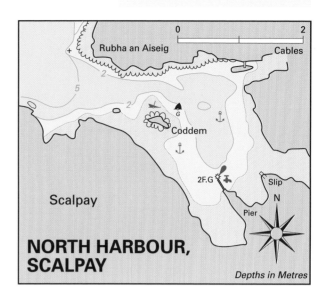

NORTH HARBOUR, SCALPAY

Depths in Metres

Lights

Lt buoy Fl.G

Supplies

Shops (including butcher), diesel, petrol, post office, telephone, water tap at pier. Harris wool and knitwear shop. Minibus to Tarbert meets ferry from the mainland.

Scalpay North Harbour

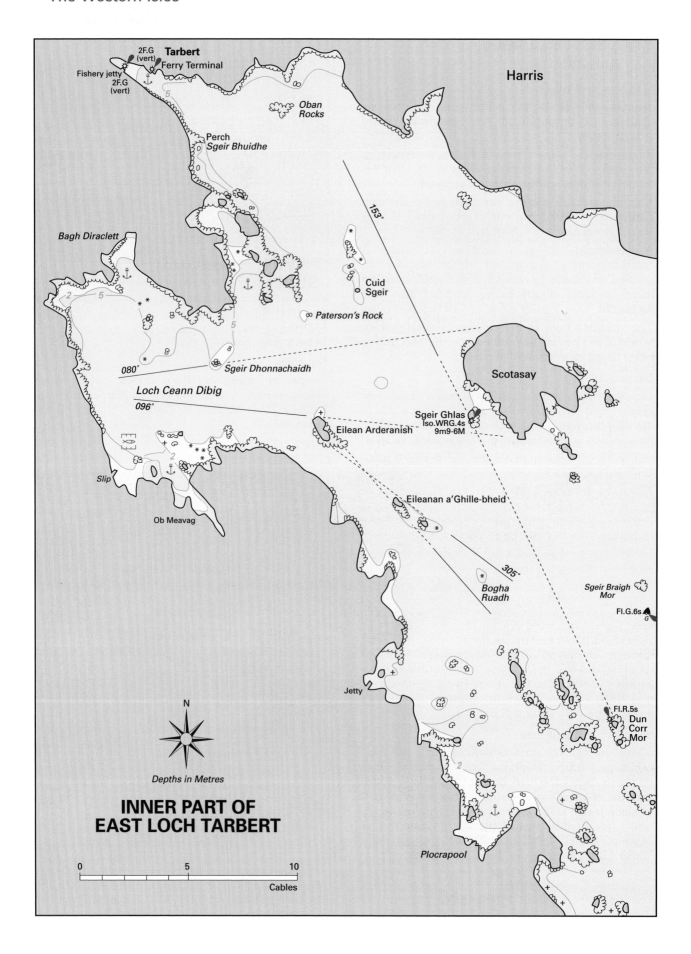

Harris

Tarbert
Ferry Terminal
2F.G (vert)
Fishery jetty
2F.G (vert)

Oban Rocks

Perch
Sgeir Bhuidhe

Bagh Diraclett

153°

Cuid Sgeir

Paterson's Rock

080°

Sgeir Dhonnachaidh

Scotasay

Loch Ceann Dibig
096°

Sgeir Ghlas
Iso.WRG.4s
9m9-6M

Eilean Arderanish

Slip

Ob Meavag

Eileanan a'Ghille-bheid

Sgeir Braigh Mor

305°

Bogha Ruadh

Fl.G.6s
G

Jetty

N

Fl.R.5s
Dun Corr Mor

Depths in Metres

**INNER PART OF
EAST LOCH TARBERT**

0   5   10

Cables

Plocrapool

Anchorages in the northwest part of East Loch Tarbert

Loch Ceann Dibig, 57°52'·5N 6°48'W, on the west side of East Loch Tarbert is obstructed by rocks on all sides but has several sheltered anchorages. The north point of Eilean Arderanish touching the south end of Scotasay 096° leads clear of all dangers to the west shore.

Ob Meavag, on the south side of Loch Ceann Dibig is shoal and drying for 2 cables from its head and drying rocks lie 2 cables northwest of the entrance, with a rock 0·9 metre high over a cable to the east, which might be mistaken for the drying rocks.

Sgeir Liath stands above water west of the entrance, with a conspicuous concrete slip beyond it, and a stone mill building south of the slip; the mill showing northwest of Sgeir Liath 210° leads close north of the drying rock.

Approach from northwest with the head of the inlet bearing 138°.

Bagh Diraclett is a shallow bay on the north side of Loch Ceann Dibig with rocks above water and drying in the approach. Little Macnab's Rock which dries 0·8 metre, the furthest southwest of these, is cleared by keeping Sgeir Dhonnachaidh, which is just above water, in line with the north side of Scotasay 080°.

Eileanan Diraclett, 57°53'N 6°47'W, are east of the north point of Loch Ceann Dibig with a sheltered anchorage on their west side. Fish cages and rocks obstruct the inner part of the inlet, but there are moderate depths to the south of them.

Tarbert village

The narrow inlet by the ferry terminal is mostly occupied by moorings and there is little space for visiting yachts. Do not anchor to ESE of a line through the pivot of the linkspan at the ferry terminal, to leave space for the ferry to manoeuvre. May be able to make fast at ferry terminal briefly to take on stores and water (not easy) but generally better to go to Scalpay and use bus.

Services and supplies

Shops, small supermarket, hardware, butcher, baker, post office, telephone, bank, hotel. Showers at Harris Hotel (beyond head of the inlet). Petrol and diesel at garage. Water at pier (not always available), also at the fishery jetty which dries on the south side of the head of the inlet. Calor Gas at Macleod Motel, beside pier. Doctor's surgery near Harris Hotel. Laundry at Harris Hotel. Car hire.

Tarbert, Harris. The inlet dries out beyond the fishery jetty in the foreground; the ferry terminal is on the left

V. Southeast Lewis

Passage notes

East Loch Tarbert to Gob na Milaid

This section of coast is as bleak and remote as any in the Outer Hebrides. There are neither roads nor houses between Loch Seaforth and Loch Shell.

There are no hazards on a direct passage between Rubha Crago or Eilean Glas and Rubh' Uisenis except for the strength of the tide, with heavy and sometimes dangerous overfalls in the Sound of Shiant.

Charts

1794, 1795 (1:100,000). OS Explorer *457* and *456* for Loch Seaforth are also strongly recommended owing to the small scale of these charts.

Tides

In the Sound of Shiant between Rubh' Uisenis and Shiant Islands the northeast-going stream begins –0305 Ullapool (+0500 Dover). The southwest-going stream begins +0320 Ullapool (–0100 Dover). The spring rate in each direction is 3 or 4 knots.

Lights

Eilean Glas LtHo Fl(3)20s43m23M
Sgeir Inoe Lt buoy Fl.G.6s
Rubh' Uisenis Lt bn Fl.5s24m11M
Shiants Lt buoy Fl.G
Gob na Milaid Fl.15s14m10M

Shelter

Eilean Hingerstay (Thinngarstaigh) in Loch Claidh and Tob Limervay in Loch Shell are easily approached in daylight.

Loch Seaforth

Waypoint mile SW of Sgeir Hal 57°54'·6N 6°39'·7W

A long narrow loch with high hills crowding in on both sides and subject to dangerous squalls from unexpected directions. The loch within is clean but there are several dangers in the approach.

Tides

Tidal streams are generally weak but reach 1 knot in the channels either side of Seaforth Island, turning at local HW and LW. At the narrows to Upper Loch Seaforth which are impassable to yachts, the streams reach 7 knots.

Constant –0016 Ullapool (–0436 Dover)

Height in metres

MHWS	MHWN	MTL	MLWN	MLWS
5·0	3·7	2·9	2·1	0·8

Dangers, marks and directions

Sgeir an Daimh, ½ mile from the shore 9 cables NNE of Rubha Crago, covers.

Sgeir Hal, in the entrance to Loch Seaforth 3 cables southwest of Rubha Bridog, the east point of the entrance, is charted as 2 metres above high water, but appears to be less, perhaps no more than 0·5 metre. Submerged reefs extend ¼ cable all round Sgeir Hal, and Sgeir Ruadh, over a cable south of Sgeir Hal, dries about 0·3 metre.

Iola Mhor, about ¼ mile SSE of Ard Caol at the west point of the entrance, dries about 0·5 metre. Sgeir Bhridag, about a cable SSE of Rubha Bridog, dries 2 metres.

Kenmore, a conspicuous promontory on the east side of Loch Seaforth 3 miles from the entrance open of the west side of the loch 341° leads east of Iola Mhor, but Sgeir an Daimh is on this line and it should not be used until past that rock.

The south point of Loch Maaruig, on the west side of Loch Seaforth opposite Kenmore, open of the east side of the loch 322°, leads west of Sgeir Bhridag.

Sgeir nan Ron, which dries 2 metres, lies 75 metres from the west shore 3 cables north of Glas Sgeir, a green islet 1¼ miles NNW of Ard Caol, and about ½ cable from the north side of a slight indentation on the west shore.

Loch Maaruig lies on the west side of Loch Seaforth 2½ miles from the entrance. Its head dries 2 cables, and a rock awash lies off a bay on the south side of Goat Point, a promontory on the north side of the loch; this rock is cleared by keeping the east end of Goat Point open of the south point of the loch, although fish cages moored there make this of academic interest at present.

Note A submerged rock lies about ¼ cable off the west end of Goat Point.

Anchor west of Goat Point.

Facilities

Telephone box at road junction 100–200m beyond head of loch. The old-style red box in a garden on the north shore is reported to be purely decorative.

Beyond Loch Maaruig the shores are less steep; Seaforth Island 2 miles further north can be passed on either side. The two bays on Harris west of the island are shoal and drying, but reasonable anchorage can be found off the jetty at Aline Lodge, northwest of Seaforth Island, or in the passage north of the island in about 7 metres, which may be more sheltered.

Two miles beyond Seaforth Island Sgeir Ghlas stands southeast of the middle of the loch with rocks which dry extending north and west from it. There is a clear passage east of Sgeir Ghlas, and the depth is reasonable for anchoring ½ mile northeast of Sgeir Ghlas in a bay on the southeast shore; a drying rock lies a cable from the southeast shore 3½ cables beyond the south point of the bay. The plan is taken from an Admiralty survey of 1850.

Three miles northeast of Seaforth Island narrows lead to Upper Loch Seaforth; the narrows are filled with drying rocks which form tidal rapids where the stream runs at up to 7 knots, with only about 5 minutes of slack water, and are not passable except in a kayak or an expendable dinghy.

Loch Claidh

57°55'N 6°36'W

The entrance lies between Eilean Mor a' Bhaigh a mile to the west, and Rubha Valamus Beag (Bhalamuis Bhig on the chart), a low rocky promontory, the most southerly point between Loch Seaforth and Rubh' Uisenis.

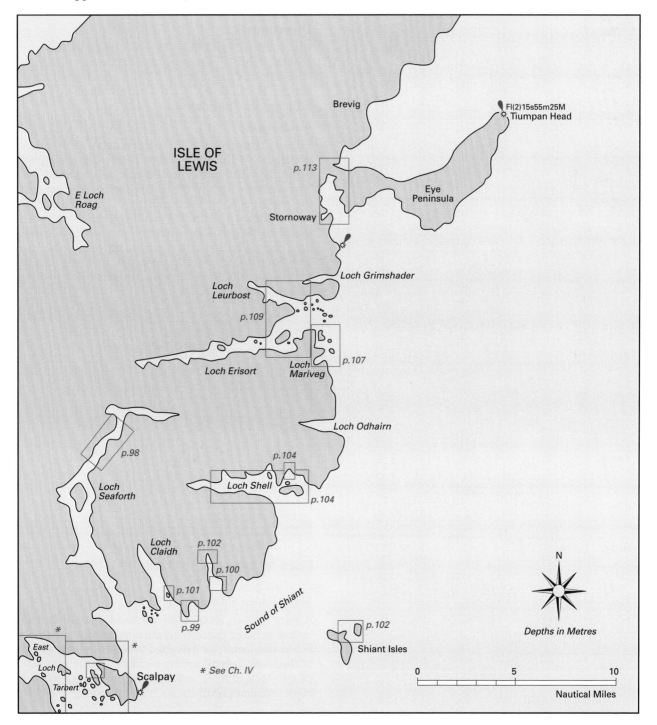

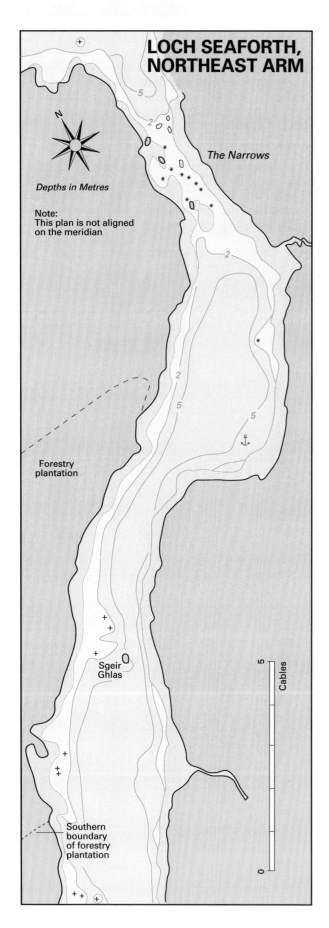

LOCH SEAFORTH, NORTHEAST ARM

N

Depths in Metres

Note:
This plan is not aligned
on the meridian

The Narrows

Forestry
plantation

Cables

Sgeir
Ghlas

Southern
boundary
of forestry
plantation

Tides

Constant −0026 Ullapool (−0446 Dover)

Height in metres

MHWS	MHWN	MTL	MLWN	MLWS
5·0	3·7	2·9	2·1	0·8

Dangers and marks

Pender Rock stands in a depth of 0·3 metre at the seaward end of a submerged reef which extends 4 cables SSE from Aird a' Bhaigh, the west point of the entrance; overfalls occur around Pender Rock. On the east side of the entrance, rocks ½ cable off Sgeir Niogag, a rock 5 metres high on a drying reef ½ mile WNW of Rubha Valamus Beag, dry up to 3·4 metres. A drying reef extends ½ cable southwest of Rubha Valamus Beag.

Directions

The south side of Eilean Mor a' Bhaigh in line with Uiseval, a hill 333 metres high on the north side of Sound of Scalpay, bearing 248°, leads close south of Pender Rock. Bring Loch Claidh well open before turning in to the entrance.

Anchorages

Eilean Hingerstay (Thinngarstaigh), 1¼ miles northwest of Rubha Valamus Beag, shelters a pool about ¾ cable across on the east side of the loch. The passage south of the island is beset by reefs, but the approach by the north of the island is straightforward. Holding and shelter have been found to be good in southerly and westerly gales, and, even in northwesterly winds, little sea comes in. Tob Smuaisibhig, on the east side of Loch Claidh 1½ miles NNW of Eilean Hingerstay, provides some shelter.

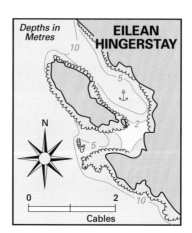

Depths in Metres — EILEAN HINGERSTAY

N

Cables

Loch Valamus (Bhalamuis)

57°55'N 6°34'W

See colour photos on page 100.

A narrow loch, shallow at the head, east of Rubha Valamus Beag, entered between that point and Sgeir Mhor Bhalamuis, a detached rock off the east point of the loch. Several drying rocks lie off the east side of the loch, and if approaching from east keep 3 cables offshore until the loch is well open.

Loch Maaruig   *Jean Lawrence*

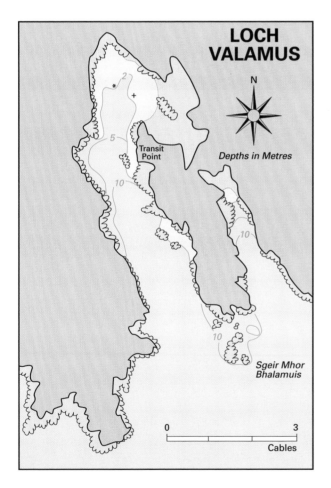

LOCH VALAMUS

N

Depths in Metres

Transit
Point

*Sgeir Mhor
Bhalamuis*

0   3

Cables

Loch Valamus

99

Loch Valamus from SE

Tob Bhrollum

About ½ mile from the entrance a pool opens up on the east side with rocks awash and drying in it. Anchor ½ cable NW of Transit Point if sufficient depth is found.

Loch Bhrollum

Waypoint 4 cables SW of Rubha Bhrollum 57°55'·4N 6°31'·6W

About 2 miles southwest of Rubh' Uisenis, Loch Bhrollum is entered between steep points off both of which drying rocks extend over ½ cable.

Aird Dubh, a grassy peninsula 15 metres high on the east side of the loch, is difficult to distinguish from the background; Meall Mor, ½ mile NNW is conspicuous.

Bogha Dubh, a group of rocks which dry 0·3 metre, lies ⅔ cable WNW of Aird Dubh.

Anchorages

Tob Bhrollum is an occasional anchorage in the bay northeast of Aird Dubh. On approaching keep 30 metres off Aird Dubh to avoid Bogha Dubh and

Head of Loch Bhrollum, Lewis

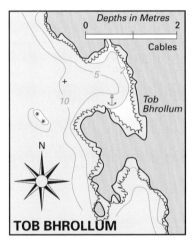

TOB BHROLLUM

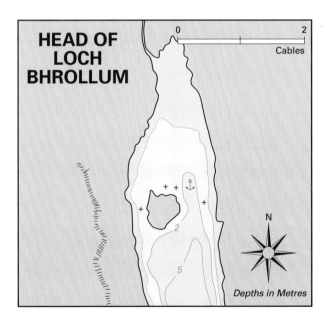

HEAD OF LOCH BHROLLUM

Tob Bhrollum from southeast

101

a reef which dries off the northwest point of Aird Dubh. A submerged rock at a depth of 0·3 metre lies nearly a cable NNW of Aird Dubh; when the west point of the entrance to Loch Bhrollum is shut in behind Aird Dubh this rock is cleared. Some swell in southerly winds may be avoided by anchoring close to the head of the bay in the southeast corner but this bay is infested with thongweed.

At the head of the loch anchor east of the islet or, at neap tides, northeast of the islet which gives better shelter from seaward than Tob Bhrollum.

Mol Mor, Shiant Isles

Shiant Isles

Waypoint ½ mile east of Eilean an Tighe 57°53'·4N 6°20'W

Tides

For tidal streams around Shiant Isles see page 960.
Constant (for Loch Shell) –0016 Ullapool (–0436 Dover)
Height in metres

MHWS	MHWN	MTL	MLWN	MLWS
4·8	3·6	2·8	1·9	0·7

A dramatic group of islands to visit in settled weather, the Shiants are usually uninhabited, although occasionally visited by shepherds. The approach from south is straightforward.

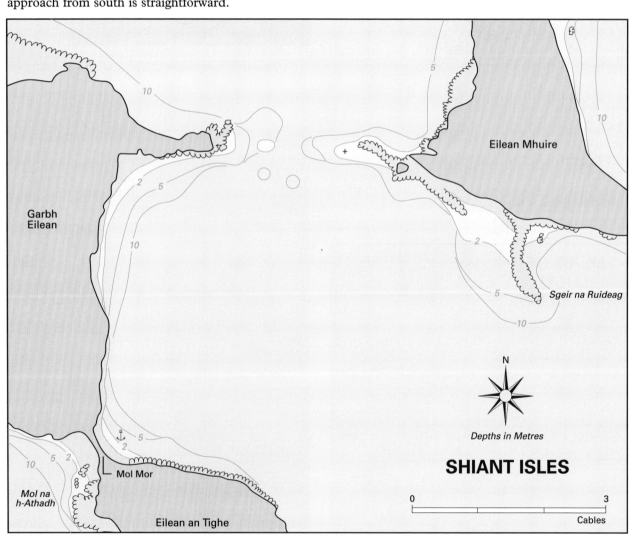

Shiant Isles

Directions

At the north side a drying reef extends 1½ cables south from a point in the western half of Eilean Mhuire, the northeast island. Another drying reef extends 1½ cables west from the same island into the passage between that island and Garbh Eilean, the northwest island, with a submerged rock at its outer end. Another drying reef extends less than ½ cable east from Garbh Eilean into the same passage. The clear passage is 1½ cables wide, but it should be taken to the west of the visible channel.

The usual anchorage in moderate westerly winds is on the east side of Mol Mor, a stony isthmus between the two western islands, but the bottom consists of boulders, with sand at greater depths further from the shore.

An alternative anchorage is the bay 3–4 cables north, where the depth is moderate and the bottom is sand with patches of weed.

In moderate easterly winds it is possible to anchor in a similar position west of Mol Mor, but there are drying rocks off its south end on that side.

Loch Shell

Waypoint 1 mile south of east end of Eilean Iuvard 57°59'N 6°25'W

The main fairway of the loch southwest of Eilean Iuvard (Iubhard) is clear of dangers, but rocks northwest of the island affect the approach to Tob Orinsay. The principal anchorage is Tob Limervay (Lemreway), north of Eilean Iuvard.

Tides

Constant –0016 Ullapool (–0436 Dover)

Height in metres

MHWS	MHWN	MTL	MLWN	MLWS
4·8	3·6	2·8	1·9	0·7

Tob Limervay

58°00'·8N 6°26'·2W

Directions

The entrance may be difficult to identify as, in some light conditions, Eilean Iuvard merges with the background.

Sgeir Phlathuig, which dries 0·9 metre, lies on the northeast side of the approach; its west side is cleared by keeping the east side of Galta Mor at the west end of the Shiant Islands in line with the southeast point of Eilean Iuvard 178° astern. The south side of the rock is cleared by keeping Rubha Buidhe in line with Sron Chrom bearing 272°.

A drying rock lies ¼ cable southwest of the east point of the entrance to Tob Limervay (on which a wooden shed stands).

Anchorage

Anchor off the east side of the inlet, taking care to leave swinging room clear of drying reefs inshore. Poor holding. Shelter in southerly winds may be found on a narrow shelf close to Eilean Iuvard south of Sgeir Fraoich.

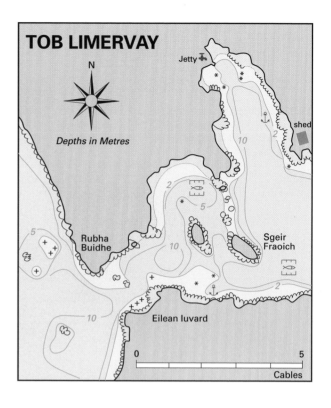

Supplies

Post office (part time), telephone, water tap beside shed at the jetty.

Dangers and marks (in the main part of Loch Shell)

Sgeir na Caorach, close southwest of the west end of Eilean Iuvard, is 1 metre high.

Sgeirean Dubha, 2 cables southwest of Rubha Buidhe, a sloping promontory on the north side of the west end of Caolas Tuath, dry 2·4 metres.

Bogha Ruadh, 2 cables WNW of Rubha Buidhe, dries 4 metres; submerged rocks lie 1 cable north and east of Bogha Ruadh.

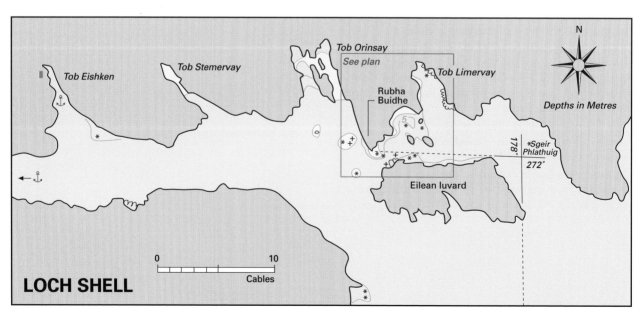

Tob Limervay

Sgeir Leum, 2 metres high, stands 4 cables WNW of Rubha Buidhe, the west point of Eilean Iuvard; a submerged rock at a depth of 0·3 metre lies ½ cable west of Sgeir Leum.

Severe gusts occur in strong winds from west and southwest in the inner part of Loch Shell. Several of the inlets are encumbered by fish cages but anchoring may still be possible.

Tob Orinsay, a mile NNW of the west end of Eilean Iuvard, lies on the west side of Orinsay Island. Between the island and a promontory on the west side the bottom appears to be shingle with a depth of 3 metres. Depth in the inlet east of the island is mostly less than 1 metre.

Tob Stemervay, 1¼ mile WNW of Eilean Iuvard, has depths of 5 metres 2 cables from the entrance.

Tob Eishken, 1½ miles from the head of the loch on the north side, has a drying rock ¾ cable from the northeast shore in the entrance; a rock awash lies ¼ cable from the west shore about 3 cables north of the west point of the entrance.

The head of the loch dries off 3 cables, and there is a reasonable area with a depth of 5–10 metres.

East coast of Lewis – Gob na Milaid to Tiumpan Head

Chart
1794 (1:100,000). OS map *14*

Tides
Tides off Kebock Head, 1½ miles north of Gob na Milaid, run at up to 3 knots at springs. The north-going stream begins −0405 Ullapool (+0400 Dover). The south-going stream begins +0220 Ullapool (−0200 Dover).

Between Kebock Head and the Eye Peninsula, east of Stornoway, the tides are weak.

Dangers and marks

The shore as far as Stornoway is free from dangers. Dubh Sgeir, a detached islet 8 metres high, stands 3 cables northeast of Torray (Eilean Thoraidh), south of the entrance to Loch Erisort.

Lights

Gob na Milaid Lt bn Fl.15s17m10M
Arnish Point Fl.WR.10s17m9/7M
Eitshal Radio Mast (58°10'·7N 6°35'W)
   4F.R(vert)237-357m
Tiumpan Head Fl(2)15s55m25M

Shelter

Loch Odhairn, Camas Orasaidh or Tob Cromore (Loch Erisort), Stornoway.

Loch Odhairn from SW

South entrance to Loch Mariveg from west

Loch Odhairn, 58°03'N 6°24'W. There are no dangers within the loch and even in easterly winds the sea rarely disturbs the inner part of the loch. Anchor east of a promontory on the south side opposite the jetty which is on the north side, a mile and a half from the entrance, to gain some shelter from westerly winds.

Supplies

Shop near jetty. Post office and telephone at Gravir, 1 mile.

Loch Mariveg (Mharabhig)

58°05'·4N 6°23'·5W

The sound behind Torray (Eilean Thoraidh) and other islands off the south side of the entrance to Loch Erisort leads to several sheltered bays and inlets around Loch Mariveg.

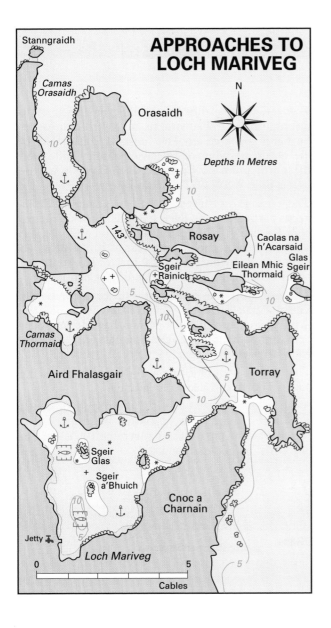

Charts

2529 (1:25,000), obsolete chart 1154 (1:14,300, depths in fathoms). OS map 14.

Tides

Constant −0010 Ullapool (−0430 Dover)
Height in metres

MHWS	MHWN	MTL	MLWN	MLWS
4·8	3·7	2·9	2·0	0·7

Dangers and marks

The passage southwest of Torray is no more than ½ cable wide and less than 2 metres deep; it is further constricted by a rock well off the shore of Torray which covers at half tide but shows white below the water.

A drying reef extends ¼ cable north of Cnoc a Charnain, the west point of the entrance.

Caolas na h'Acarsaid, the passage between Rosay (Eilean Rosaidh) and Eilean Mhic Thormaid, the island north of Torray, is identified by Dubh Sgeir, an 8-metre islet ¼ mile east of the larger islands.

An uncharted rock at a depth of 1·2 metres lies ¼ cable southeast of Rosay, and a submerged reef extends ½ cable north of Sgeir Rainich at the inner end of the passage.

Directions

On entering from seaward keep in the southern third of the channel between Eilean Mhic Thormaid and Rosay until north of the former island, then mid-channel, and towards the west end of the passage keep north of mid-channel until the north pool opens up.

Anchorages

Loch Mariveg is obstructed by several rocks above water and drying, and fish cages are moored along much of the west side of the loch. A submerged reef has been found between Sgeir a' Bhuic and Sgeir Ghlas.

The best anchorages are southeast of Sgeir a' Bhuic and in the northwest corner.

The jetty in the southwest corner dries; there is a water tap at the head of the jetty and a telephone nearby.

Torray, on its west side, east of lines of buoys of mussel farms there and clear of drying reefs which extend 50 metres southeast of an islet there.

Aird Fhalasgair, in the bay ¼ mile south of the point. A drying rock lies ¼ cable off the south point of the bay.

Camas Thormaid (known to local yachtsmen as the Witches' Pool), northwest of Aird Fhalasgair. Keep 20 metres from the south shore to avoid a drying rock 60 metres off, and anchor southwest of the 20-metre islet, where the bottom is heavy clay. There are submerged rocks north of the drying rock.

In the basin south or southwest of Orasaidh. A drying rock ¾ cable from the west shore is cleared by keeping the west side of Sgeir Rainich in line the east side of Cnoc a Charnain 143°.

Caolas na h'Acarsaid from NE. Loch Mariveg is at upper left

Loch Erisort

Waypoint ½ mile SSE of Tabhaidh Mhor 58°06'·6N 6°22'·3W

The shores of Loch Erisort and Loch Leurbost are fringed with scattered settlements, and several bays are suitable for anchoring.

Tides

Tidal streams are insignificant.
Constant –0010 Ullapool (–0430 Dover)
Height in metres

	MHWS	MHWN	MTL	MLWN	MLWS
	4·8	3·7	2·9	2·0	0·7

Dangers and marks

Tavay islands, Tabhaidh Mhor and Tabhaidh Bheag, stand in the middle of the entrance.

Barkin Islands, of which the main island is Tannaraidh, stand in the mouth of Loch Leurbost, northwest of Tavay.

Sgeirean Dubha Tannaraidh, a reef above water and drying, lie over a cable southwest of Tannaraidh, with a channel 10 metres deep between the reef and Tannaraidh.

Tanneray (note different spelling on the chart to distinguish from Tannaraidh, above; to confuse us further it appeared on older charts as Eilean Glas) at the northeast point of Eilean Chaluim Chille, and the north point of Cromore anchorage, is a little over a mile WSW of Tabhaidh Bheag.

The passage northwest of Eilean Chaluim Chille needs particular care: Sgeir nan Lus, a rock 2 metres high 1½ cables NNE of Eilean Chaluim Chille, has a drying reef ½ cable southwest of it. Plaideag, an extensive reef which dries 2·9 metres lies southeast of mid-channel, 3 cables beyond Sgeir nan Lus.

The islets on the northwest side of the passage, Eilean Chalaibrigh on which is an inconspicuous light beacon, and Eilean a' Bhlair, have drying rocks between them although there is a passage 1½ cables wide between the rocks.

The passage west of Eilean a' Bhlair is clear, as is the passage north of Eilean Chalaibrigh.

A submerged rock lies about ½ cable south of Eilean a' Bhlair. Transits can be picked off the chart or sketch plan to pass these dangers and it is best to plot them before approaching.

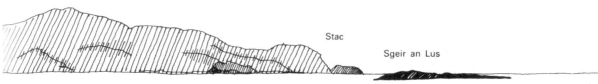

Leading line 060° – Loch Erisort

108

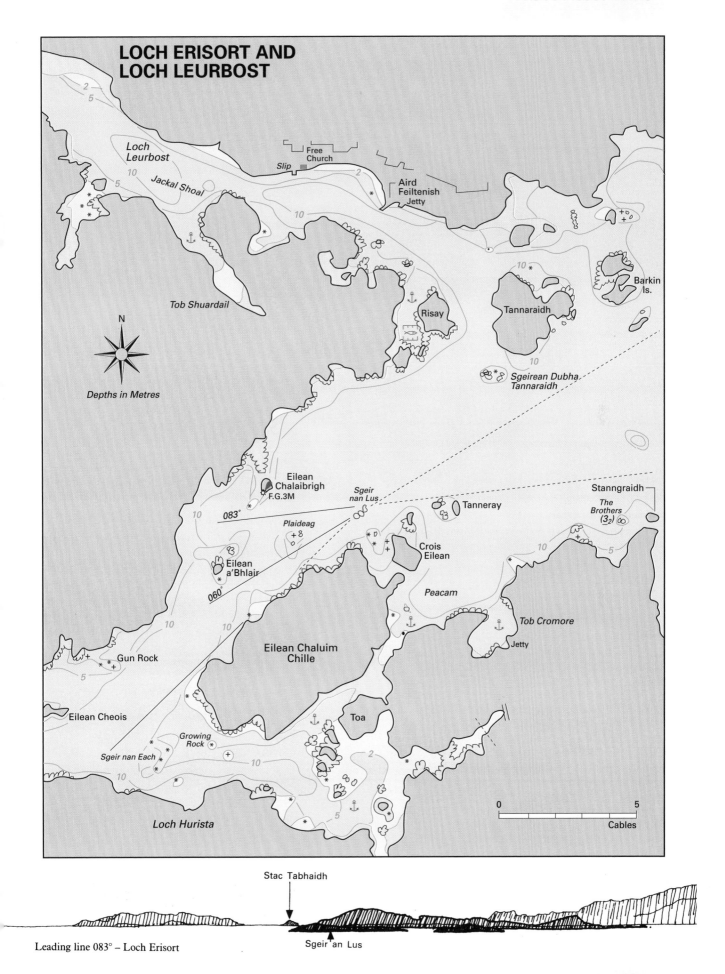

LOCH ERISORT AND LOCH LEURBOST

Loch Leurbost

Jackal Shoal

Free Church

Slip

Aird Feiltenish Jetty

Barkin Is.

Tob Shuardail

Risay

Tannaraidh

N

Depths in Metres

Sgeirean Dubha Tannaraidh

Eilean Chalaibrigh
F.G.3M

Sgeir nan Lus

Tanneray

Stanngraidh

The Brothers (3₂)

083°

Plaideag

Crois Eilean

Eilean a'Bhlair

060°

Peacam

Tob Cromore

Jetty

Eilean Chaluim Chille

Gun Rock

Eilean Cheois

Toa

Growing Rock

Sgeir nan Each

0   5
Cables

Loch Hurista

Stac Tabhaidh

Leading line 083° – Loch Erisort

Sgeir an Lus

109

Barkin Isles, Loch Erisort

Camas Orasaidh from south, showing the boat passage at high water

Sgeir nan Lus in line with Stac Tabhaidh, south of Tabhaidh Mhor 083° leads north of Plaideag, as well as through the passage between Chalaibrigh and Eilean a' Bhlair.

Sgeir nan Lus in line with a 13-metre Stac at the north point of the entrance to Loch Erisort 060° leads southeast of Plaideag, which is the most straightforward course to take at this point.

Lights
Tabhaidh Bheag Fl.3s13m3M 260°-obscd-295°
Eilean Chalaibrigh Fl.G.5m3M

Anchorages
Camas Orasaidh 58°06'·5N 6°23'·8W, is between Eilean Orasaidh and Stanngraidh, the south point of the entrance to Loch Erisort. The depth is 6 metres close to head of the inlet, which connects by a shallow, boulder-strewn channel at high water with the passages leading to Loch Mariveg (see pages 107-110).

Peacam (Cromore) 58°06'·5N 6°25'W, on the east side of Eilean Chaluim Chille. On the south side of the approach the Brothers, a rock about a cable west of Stanngraidh, dries 3·2 metres. Anchor south of Sgeir Peacam.

Tob Cromore, an enclosed basin on the southeast side of Peacam, has a depth of 2–3 metres over most of its area, with a few moorings for inshore fishing boats, leaving plenty of space to anchor. A drying rock lies on the northwest side of the basin.

Water tap at the jetty, which dries; the southwest face is the most convenient to go alongside.

Anchorages in the inner part of the loch
Loch Hurista (Thorasdaidh) 58°06'N 6°26'W, south of Eilean Chaluim Chille.

Rocks dry ½ cable southwest of Eilean Chaluim Chille, and Sgeir nan Each, a reef about a cable across with several rocks which dry on it, lies a cable from the south shore.

A rock which dries 3·2 metres lies about cable from the south shore a cable ESE of the south end of Sgeir nan Each.

Growing Rock ¾ cable southwest of Eilean Chaluim Chille dries 1·7 metres, and a submerged rock lies in mid-channel ¾ cable ESE of Growing Rock.

Directions
The most easterly rock of Sgeir nan Each is charted as drying 4·2 metres; if it can be identified without doubt, pass at least a cable west of Eilean Chaluim Chille then steer to pass ½ cable east of the rock which dries 4·2 metres until near the south shore and then turn to head for the anchorage chosen.

Cromore Bay, Lewis, from south

Tob Cromore from southeast

Otherwise keep Sgeir nan Lus in sight astern until close to the south shore and turn to follow the south shore eastwards keeping ¼ cable off the shore until past Rubh' an Tanga, its most northerly point.

Anchor in the passage southeast of Eilean Chaluim Chille or pass south and east of the islets in the middle of Loch Hurista and anchor south of Toa, a peninsula in the northeast corner of the loch. Drying rocks lie up to ¾ cable off the southwest side of the loch.

Keose, 58°06'N 6°29'W, stands on the north shore 1 mile west of Eilean Chaluim Chille. The channel north of Eilean Cheois is navigable, although there are several fish cages. Gun Rock and a reef, part of which uncovers, extends a cable ESE from the north shore NNE of Eilean Cheois. Anchor southwest of the jetty in the northwest corner of the bay.

Loch Erisort is navigable for a further 3 miles and several bays on either shore are suitable for anchoring. A rock ½ cable off the north shore ¾ mile west of Keose dries 0·2 metre. Two miles west of Keose two rocks above water stand on a drying reef which extends up to 1½ cables from the south shore. Bogh' a' Chaolais which dries 1·7 metres lies a cable north of these rocks.

Supplies

At Ballallan at the head of the loch.

Loch Leurbost

58°08'N 6°25'W

Dangers

Sgeirean Dubha Tannaraidh is a drying reef with a rock 2 metres high about a cable southwest of Tannaraidh. A rock 1 cable from the north shore 1 cable NNW of Tannaraidh covers at HWS.

Directions

Loch Leurbost may be entered either by the north or southwest side of Tannaraidh. The loch narrows to less than 1 cable 1 mile from Tannaraidh; Jackal Shoal, 1 cable northwest of the south point of the narrows has a depth of 1·8 metres over it.

Anchorages

Risay, the basin west of Risay, on the south side of the entrance to Loch Leurbost, has depths of 2–3 metres, soft mud, and can only be entered from the north.

Tob Shuardail on the south side of the loch, immediately west of the narrows. Jackal Shoal, on the south side of the narrows lies at a depth of 1·8 metres.

Head of the loch south of Orasaigh; the head of the loch is shoal for about 3 cables.

Off the jetty at Aird Feiltenish, or off the slip beside the Free Church at Crossbost. Many moorings. Bus to Stornoway. No supplies.

Loch Grimshader

58°09'N 6°23'W

Sgeir a' Chaolais which dries 3·7 metres lies south of mid-channel about ¾ mile inside the loch opposite a bay on the north side. The south point of the entrance kept in sight open of the south shore 102° clears this rock. In the southwest branches of the loch the bottom is soft mud.

Loch Beag, the northwest arm, is crossed by a power cable with a safe clearance of 12 metres.

Stornoway Harbour

Waypoint 3 cables SE of Arnish Point LH 58°11'·2N 6°21'·6W

A sheltered natural harbour with heavy fishing-boat and ferry traffic and little shelter for a yacht free from disturbance. Most services and supplies are available, but yachts have to take their chance with the fishing boats. Under the bye-laws all anchors must be buoyed and the harbourmaster has authority to have a boat moved.

A new ferry terminal has been built extending 200° from the east shore of the Outer Harbour.

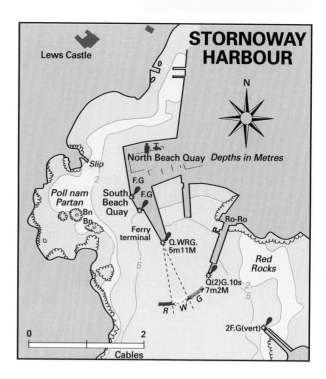

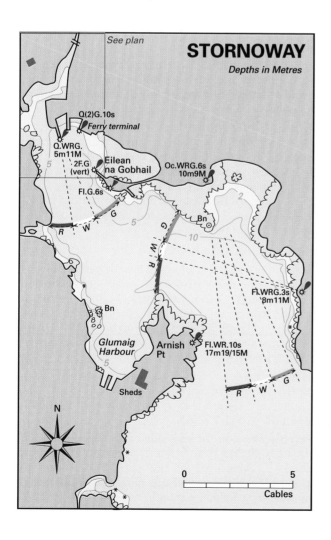

Chart

2529 (1:25,000 and 1:10,000); OS Explorer *459*

Tides

Tidal streams are negligible but seiches, which are rapid rises or falls of 0·5 metre in 10 minutes, occur usually during unsettled weather.

Constant −0010 Ullapool (−0430 Dover)

Height in metres

MHWS	MHWN	MTL	MLWN	MLWS
4·8	3·7	2·9	2·0	0·7

Dangers and marks

The sheds at Arnish Point are conspicuous.

Chicken Rock, 3 miles ESE of Arnish Point and about ¼ mile SW of Chicken Head, 5 metres high with a beacon with a spherical topmark, is marked by a S cardinal light buoy.

The Beasts of Holm are rocks a cable SSE of Holm Point at the east side of the entrance which dry up to 2·3 metres and are marked by a green beacon 5 metres high.

A NATO fuel jetty is prominent on the west side of Branahuie Bay, about 1½ miles east of Arnish Point.

Drying reefs extend up to a cable northeast of Arnish Point, marked by a red can light buoy, and up to a cable north of the northwest part of the point, marked by a metal framework beacon 5 metres high near its outer end, although this may have collapsed.

Drying reefs extend up to a cable from the east shore; Sgeir Mhor Inaclete extends 2 cables from the north shore opposite Arnish Point, marked by a beacon 5 metres high near the outer end.

Beyond this, there are no dangers in the fairway.

Lights

Arnish Point Fl.WR.10s17m9/7M

Stornoway Harbour from southwest. Poll nam Partan on left

NATO Fuel Jetty (about 1½ miles east of Arnish Point) 2F.R(vert).
Sandwick Oc.WRG.6s10m9M
Stoney Field Fl.WRG.3s8m11M
Eilean na Gobhail Fl.G.6s8m
Slip jetty, NW end of Eilean na Gobhail 2F.G(vert)
No.1 Pier Q.WRG.5m11M
New ferry terminal Q(2)G.10s
Chicken Rock Lt buoy Q(6)+LFl.15s

At night

Approach in the white sector of Arnish Point light and in turn the white sector of Sandwick light beacon, the white sector of Stoney Field light beacon astern, and the white sector of the light at No.1 Pier.

Anchorages

A new pontoon with access bridge has been installed at the north end of Inner Harbour with eight berths for visitors, maximum size 12 metres. Security fence and entrance gate operated by key card, available at the harbour office. Fresh water, electricity and rubbish bin at entrance gate. Harbour office listens Ch 16 and Ch 12, 24 hours a day. Call harbour office for berthing instructions.

Anchorages are all subject to disturbance from passing traffic, especially on Friday and Sunday nights.

Poll nam Partan has drying rocks well off the southwest side marked by lattice beacons with spherical topmarks. Most of the space is taken up with private and lifeboat moorings. If anchoring, avoid swinging into the fairway. Holding reported to be poor.

Glumaig Harbour, west of Arnish Point, is sheltered but the industrial surroundings and the distance from the town detract from it. A drying reef on the west side of the entrance is marked by a green beacon with a cage topmark, and other drying rocks lie ¾ cable south of the beacon. The bottom is foul with scrap steel and discarded equipment and the anchor should be buoyed.

Services and supplies

Shops, post office, telephone, hotels, bank. Showers at Fishermen's Mission on quay or Nicholson Sports Centre (also swimming baths). Petrol at garage, water and diesel at North Beach Quay. Fishermen's chandlery at North Beach Quay. Supermarket near ferry terminal and Calor Gas at McIvers nearby. Car hire. Doctor.

Harbourmaster VHF Ch 12 (24-hour watch)
☎ 01851 702688
Coastguard station is in a new building at Battery Point ☎ 01851 702013

Bayble Bay, on the east side of the Eye Peninsula, provides shelter from westerly winds in 10 metres, about 2 cables SE of the pier. Yachts can go alongside the pier at half tide. The end of the pier is marked by a reflective panel.

Brevig Harbour

Submerged rocks lie on the line of the pier, and it should be approached with the face of the pier slightly open.

PO in Lower Bayble ½M, shop at Upper Bayble, ½M.

The coast north of Tiumpan Head is described in Chapter VI as it is only likely to be of interest to a yacht on passage round the Butt of Lewis.

Brevig Harbour 58°16'·1N 06°17'·5W

A new harbour, opened in November 1995, on the west side of Broad Bay, west of the Eye Peninsula. The entrance, 20m wide, faces approximately south, with a double dog-leg leading to an inner basin 50m x 30m..

McIver Rock, awash in the middle of Broad Bay, is clear south of the approach.

Lights

2F.R(vert) on the W side of the entrance
2F.G(vert) on the E side of the entrance
Fresh water and fuel are available alongside.

VI. West side of the Outer Hebrides

The Atlantic coast of the Outer Hebrides has little shelter and in heavy westerly weather it would be dangerous to run for any of the passages between the islands, especially with a west-going tide when there would be heavy overfalls at the entrance to each sound. In clear visibility some of the lochs on the west side of Lewis provide accessible shelter. Strong tides and heavy seas occur off both Barra Head and Butt of Lewis.

For through passages between islands south of Barra see Chapter I.

The west side of Barra and the Uists

Charts

2769 and *2770* (1:30,000) cover the west coast of Barra with the passages through the sounds. Chart *2722* (1:200,000) gives small-scale coverage from Skerryvore to St Kilda, but Imray chart *C66* (1:150,000), perhaps used in conjunction with OS map *31*, is sufficient for a passage along this coast, although there are many hazards. OS Explorer *452* covers Barra and *453* covers South Uist. *454* covers North Uist.

The distance from Flodday, at the northwest end of Sound of Pabbay to Monach Isles is 37 miles.

Sound of Vatersay

Several dangerous rocks lie up to ½ mile west of the entrance and the leading line is not easily distinguished. The traditional line is two houses on Vatersay in line 135°; the front house is stone-coloured, the rear one has a red roof and a road runs close northeast of them. Once within the entrance steer for the 50-metre hill east of the rear house to avoid Bo Leahan on the southwest side of the line. A slip is to be built into the west side of the new causeway.

There are no hazards on a direct line between Vatersay Sound and Greian Head at the northwest of Barra.

For the passage through the Sound of Barra see Chapter I.

Dangers and marks

Off the west side of South Uist drying rocks extend up to a mile from the shore and at the north end of

South Uist Ardivachar Rocks which dry 3·2 metres are 1½ miles from the shore. The 20-metre contour avoids these dangers by a reasonable margin. Rubha Ardvule, 7 metres high, which lies 8 miles north of the Sound of Barra, is prominent.

All timings are UTC. All positions are related to WGS84 datum.

An inshore danger area extends 20 miles seaward from 2 miles south of Rubha Ardvule to Ardivachar Point and is in frequent use for short range live firing trials throughout the year Monday to Saturday, 1000–1800hrs, this period may be extended to 2359hrs on Tuesdays and Thursdays. Red flashing beacons Iso.R.2s visible by day and flags (red lamps by night) are illuminated and hoisted one hour before live activity commences. The flags are situated at prominent locations throughout the Range. The red flashing beacons are located at North Vedette 57°23'N 07°25'W height 3 metres, Falconet Tower 57°22'N 07°24'W height 15 metres and Range Main Entrance 57°21'N 07°22'W height 9 metres. A Range Safety vessel patrols the actual inshore danger areas when activity is in progress.

An extended range is used for long-range live firing trials. Firing trials will be conducted within discrete areas bounded by the west coast of South Uist out to 11°40'W between 56°25'N and 58°30'N. Stornoway Coast Guard will broadcast a navigational warning whenever this extended Range is in use.

A daily Range activity and inshore weather forecast is broadcast on VHF marine Ch 73 after making an alerting call on Ch 12 (local fishing channel). The broadcast is normally made at

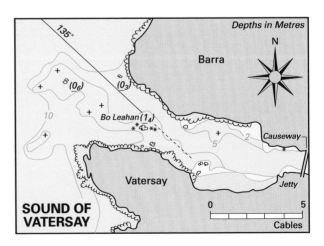

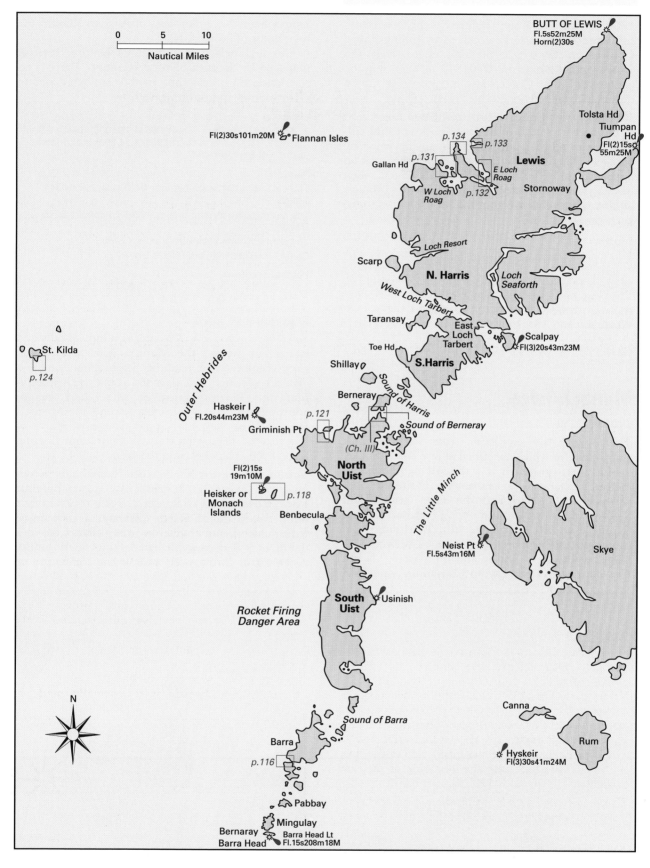

0   5   10
Nautical Miles

BUTT OF LEWIS
Fl.5s52m25M
Horn(2)30s

Tolsta Hd
Tiumpan Hd
Fl(2)15s
55m25M

Fl(2)30s101m20M ☼ Flannan Isles

p.134
p.133
p.131
Gallan Hd
E Loch Roag
Lewis
W Loch Roag
p.132
Stornoway

Loch Resort

Scarp

Loch Seaforth

N. Harris

West Loch Tarbert

St. Kilda
p.124

Taransay

Toe Hd
East Loch Tarbert
Scalpay
Fl(3)20s43m23M

Outer Hebrides

S.Harris

Shillay

Berneray
Sound of Harris

Haskeir I
Fl.20s44m23M ☼
Griminish Pt
p.121
Sound of Berneray

(Ch. III)

Fl(2)15s
19m10M
North Uist
Heisker or Monach Islands
p.118

The Little Minch

Benbecula

Neist Pt ☼
Fl.5s43m16M
Skye

Rocket Firing Danger Area

South Uist
Usinish ☼

N

Canna

Sound of Barra

Barra
Rum

p.116

Hyskeir
☼ Fl(3)30s41m24M

Pabbay

Bernaray
Barra Head
Mingulay
Barra Head Lt
Fl.15s208m18M

St Kilda Peak 352° distant about 3 miles

1000hrs or 1 hour before Range activity. Information may also be obtained by calling Range Control on ☎ 01870 604535, alternatively the Guardroom (24hrs) on ☎ 01870 604535 may be contacted. Range Control also monitor VHF Ch 16 during all trial activity.

Bo Ruag which dries 1·2 metres, lies 3 miles west of the northwest end of Benbecula, close to the 20-metre line, and its position is usually revealed by breakers. There is no clearing mark for this rock on a passage along the coast and the best course when heading north is to steer for the disused lighthouse at Shillay at the west end of the Monach Isles, or to keep closer inshore.

Lights

New lights make some contribution to navigation in this area, as follows:

Monach Is at old LtHo 57°31'·6N 7°41'·6W White framework tower Fl(2)15s19m10M

Haskeir (57°42'N 7°41'·3W) Fl.20s23M

Whale Rock (57°54'·9N 8°00'·7W) E card pillar buoy Q(3)10s.

Gasker 57°54'·9N 7°17'·2W

Monach Isles

57°31'N 7°38'W

The Monach Isles consist of Ceann Ear, Shivinish and Ceann Iar which are joined at low water; Shillay to the west, on which is a disused lighthouse 40 metres high, with a reasonably sheltered pool between that island and the main group, and Stockay which stands on a drying reef northeast of Ceann Ear. Rocks above water, drying and submerged are scattered over an area between 2½ miles northwest of Shillay and the coast of North Uist northeast of Stockay, to Causamul, which is 8

metres high, 1½ miles west of Aird an Runair, the west point of North Uist.

This archipelago is a National Nature Reserve, managed by Scottish Natural Heritage. There is no restriction on access, but visitors are asked not to disturb birds and not to leave litter.

Charts

2722 (1:200,000). Imray chart C66 (1:150,000) (best). OS maps 22, 18. Obsolete chart 2805 (1:24,300) is extremely useful. OS Explorer 454

Tides

The north-going stream begins –0420 Ullapool (+0345 Dover)

The south-going stream begins +0205 Ullapool (–0215 Dover)

The spring rate in each direction is 2 knots.

Constant –0103 Ullapool (–0523 Dover)

Height in metres

MHWS	MHWN	MTL	MLWN	MLWS
4·2	3·0	2·4	1·3	0·4

Dangers and marks

They are too numerous to mention individually and navigation around the Monach Isles depends on good visibility as some of the clearing marks are at a distance of more than 10 miles. It may be helpful to plot the leading lines on the chart before approaching. The whole area around the Monach Isles and the west end of the Sound of Harris is strewn with fishing tackle with buoys and floating lines, up to 10 miles from the land.

Sound of Monach lies between Stockay and North Uist, but its navigable width is reduced by East Rock, 6 cables east of Stockay, drying rocks up to 2 miles southwest of North Uist and a submerged rock (which is not shown on Imray chart C66) at a depth of 1·8 metres further southwest, 1½ miles northeast of Stockay. A leading line for Sound of

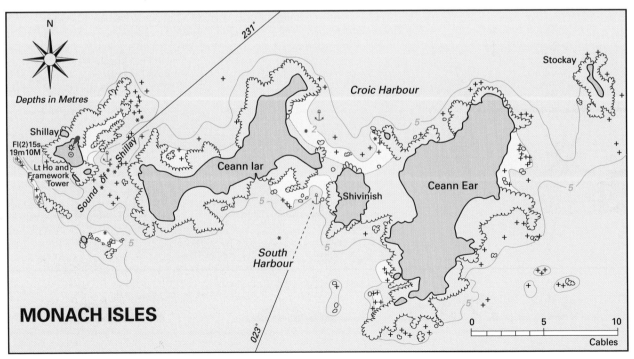

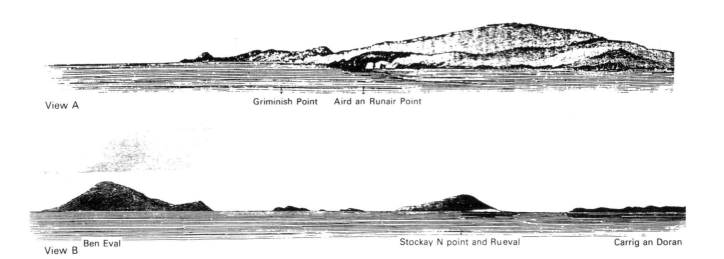

View A   Griminish Point   Aird an Runair Point

View B   Ben Eval   Stockay N point and Rueval   Carrig an Doran

Monach is the west side of Causamul under the west part of Haskeir 333°.

Charlotte Rocks, parts of which dry, south of Causamul are close west of this line and the usual passage north is Sound of Causamul for which the leading line is Griminish Point just open of Aird an Runair 029°, see View A above.

Deasker, 3 metres high, about 2 miles north of Ceann Ear, is prominent.

In the passage west of Shillay drying reefs extend ½ mile south and ¼ mile west of Shillay, and the southeast end of Huskeran an extensive drying reef lies 9 cables northwest of Shillay. Ray Sgeir, 6 metres high which lies ½ mile south of Shillay, is a useful reference mark.

Shillay, Monach Is, from WSW. The Eternal Isles beacons are at the extreme right; the drying rocks in the entrance to the Sound of Shillay are above and left of the lighthouse

John's North Channel to the northwest of Monach Isles is the other main channel among all these hazards, and would be taken by a boat on a passage between Monach Isles and St Kilda. The leading line for John's North Channel is the north point of Stockay in line with Rueval, the highest hill on Benbecula 116°, see View B.

West Dureberg, a reef – parts of which dry – lies between ½–1 mile north of Huskeran, an extensive reef 1½ miles northwest of Shillay. Clearing marks for West Dureberg are the northeast point of Ceann Ear in line with Rueval 114°, and Ray Sgeir in line with the west side of Shillay 157°, although this leads very close to West Dureberg.

The dangers described by no means exhaust the inventory, and such charts as there are should be studied carefully.

Anchorages

Anchorages at Monach Isles are used by lobster fishermen, some of whom have laid moorings there, and creels are left with buoys attached. The islands may be approached by any of the channels described above; from Sound of Causamul pass east of Deasker, 3 metres high, which is nearly 2 miles north of Ceann Ear.

Sound of Shillay, the best anchorage at the Monach Isles, lies between Shillay and Ceann Iar. It is entered from northeast between Edward Rock which dries 3·4 metres at the end of a reef ¼ mile north of the west point of Ceann Iar, and Stallion Rock which dries 2·1 metres 4 cables northeast of Shillay; other rocks lie up to 3 cables NNW of Stallion Rock. Stone beacons 4 metres high on Eilean Siorruidh (Eternal Isles), which are 1½ cables ESE of the disused lighthouse, in line 231° lead in to Sound of Shillay. In westerly winds, anchor in Poll Bane east of the jetty but the bottom shoals abruptly from 7 metres to less than 2 metres about a cable off the jetty.

A light, Fl(3)15s15m10M has been installed on a framework tower beside the 'disused lighthouse' on Shillay, Monach Isles

Croic Harbour, the bay on the north side of the main islands, provides shelter from east to northwest with a bottom of sand, but with clay in places, and isolated rocks in depths of less than 2 metres.

South Harbour lies between the south side of Ceann Iar and the west side of Shivinish. Several drying rocks lie up to ½ mile from the shores of each island; approach with middle of the isthmus between Ceann Iar and Shivinish bearing 023°.

The entrance to Griminish Harbour from north. Sgeir Dubh Mor at lower right, Callernish House at upper right

Passage notes – Causamul to Pabbay

Charts
2841 (1:50,000) and 2642 (1:30,000) cover Sound of Pabbay etc; OS Explorer 454

Dangers and marks
Pabbay lies at the west end of Sound of Harris, 14 miles northeast of Causamul. Boreray is 3 miles southwest of Pabbay and Spuir, 12 metres high, lies a mile north of Boreray. The clearest course between Griminish Point and the Sound of Harris is outside Pabbay and through the Sound of Shillay.

Bo Lea which is awash, lies 1½ miles offshore 3 miles northeast of Griminish Point. Causamul in line with Griminish Point 221° and Spuir in line with the southeast side of Pabbay 058° lead northwest of Bo Lea.

To pass south of Pabbay, use these transits to clear Bo Lea then pass north of Spuir, and head for the north side of Berneray. Bo Leac Caolas, which seems to extend further than the chart shows and dries about 0·5 metre, lies in the middle of the Sound of Pabbay.

When within ½–1 mile of Berneray steer for the north tip of Ensay bearing about 060° to avoid a shoal spit which extends ½ mile north of Berneray.

Griminish Harbour

Waypoint 57°40'·5N 7°27'W

Charts
The edition of chart 2841 published in 1998 was extended to Griminish, and it would be unwise to attempt a passage in this area without this chart.

Valley Sound, the shallow inlet west of Vallay, a tidal island, is used as a base for lobster fishing boats during the summer, but the sound is obstructed by drying rocks. The plan and the directions are based on information provided by Calum Macleod, the harbourmaster for the Western Isles Council, as well as John Stewart of Kallin who works a fishing boat from Griminish. The entrance can be difficult to discern, and if it is necessary to attempt it, approach at half tide or above, as follows.

Dangers and marks
When bearing about 200° Callernish House, a conspicuous single-storey house, circular in plan, stands in line with a hollow of the hills in the background, with a conspicuous mast to the right of the hollow.

Sgeir Dubh Mor, a rock above water, stands on a drying reef 2 cables offshore north of Callernish House. An orange float is tied to the remains of a former light beacon on Sgeir Dubh Mor.

Drying rocks lie up to ½ mile offshore north of the west end of Vallay. *Vallay* light beacon (inconspicuous) stands on the west side of the northwest end of Vallay, with a painted rock on the

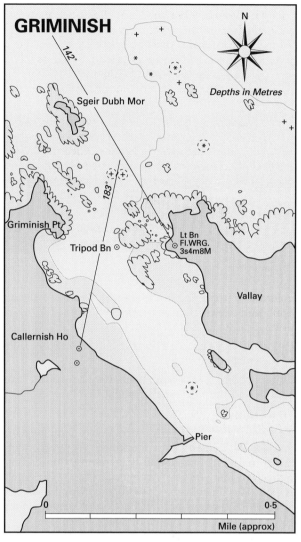

foreshore in line with the light beacon, leads between Dubh Sgeir Mor and these rocks.

Rocks with a clear channel 20 metres wide between them lie between the end of Vallay and Sgeir Dubh Mor. Beacons east of Callernish House, BW

Griminish; looking out to seaward on the leading line at LWS. Seas are breaking on the rocks between which the line leads

Griminish Pier

columns with diamond topmarks, in line bearing 183° lead between these rocks.

Drying reefs extend 1 cable west of Vallay with a tripod beacon on a rock southwest of Eilean Na Luis at the west edge.

Other drying rocks and sanbanks lie within the sound, and the tide runs strongly.

Directions
Keep north of 57°40'·5N until Vallay light beacon and the Painted Rock are identified. Approach with these marks in line about 142°. Bring the leading lights into line 183° to pass between two submerged rocks. This line leads close to the tripod beacon, after which turn towards Vallay Sound keeping close to the southwest foreshore of Vallay Island.

Many floats mark the moorings of the local fishing fleet and good sheltered anchorage can be found.

Lights
Vallay Fl.WRG.3s4m8M
Ldg Lts 183° Q.G.6/7m4M
Jetty on southwest shore 2F.G(vert) April–October

Services
Fuel and mains electricity at the pier; 1-ton crane; no water at present.

East end of Vallay The *Admiralty Pilot* notes an anchorage south of the east end of Vallay, which is shown on the new edition of chart *2841*; drying reefs lie at either side of the entrance.

Caolas a' Mhorain (Ardavuran Channel)
This channel is the approach to Sound of Berneray between Boreray and Ardavuran (Aird a' Mhorain), a mile to the southwest.

Gairgrada, a mile west of Ardavuran dries 1·8 metres. To clear Gairgrada and reefs off Ardavuran steer with Boreray touching Leac Bhan on North Uist 095°, then the summit of Lingay under Beinn Mhor 123°.

The area south and east of Boreray is shoal but that island does provide some shelter from the swell. Boreray makes an interesting excursion in quiet weather, anchoring on sand in the bay on the east side of the island.

Sound of Pabbay, with Sound of Spuir, provides the most direct course between the west side of Uist and the Sound of Harris, but Sound of Shillay north of Pabbay is clean and should be taken in poor visibility or if there is any doubt about identifying various hazards.

Spuir, 2 miles southwest of Pabbay, is 12 metres high. Reefs and detached drying rocks extend ¼ mile south of Spuir and McIver Rocks, which dry 3 metres, lie nearly a mile east.

Spuir Reef, halfway between Spuir and Pabbay, is shown on older charts as drying, but, in fact, it rarely uncovers.

Shoal sand spits and drying rocks extend at least ½ mile from Pabbay and Berneray, and a rock which dries 0·5 metre, Bo Leac Caolas, lies in the middle of Sound of Pabbay.

No leading marks are known for this passage.

Sound of Berneray
A causeway has been constructed between North Uist and Berneray, so there is no longer a way through the Sound of Berneray, and the channels on the west side will probably silt up or, at the least, change.

Flannan Isles from west   *Gillian Smith*

122

St Kilda

57°48'N 8°35'W

The St Kilda group of islands, 42 miles west of Pabbay at the west end of Sound of Harris, is designated a World Heritage Site. The main island was inhabited until 1930 and is now owned by the National Trust for Scotland (NTS), leased to Scottish Natural Heritage (SNH). Apart from the area used by the QuinetiQ MoD Hebrides Ranges, the island is managed by a warden on behalf of NTS and SNH, who lives at the 'Factor's House', a white house just above the range buildings. The warden's permission must be obtained to go beyond the village.

Visibility and weather suitable for visiting St Kilda do not occur frequently and a yacht must be prepared to clear out at short notice. For passages through Sound of Harris see Chapter III.

Access to the islands is subject to comprehensive bye-laws, displayed on a notice board at the pier. These should be studied, and in particular they prohibit the landing of dogs, introduction of alien plant or animal species, and removal or damage of any plants, bird, or animal from the islands.

Charts

2721 (1:200,000) or *2720* if coming from south; plan on *2524* (1:25,000). OS map *18*.

Tides

Around St Kilda the northeast-going stream begins +0545 Ullapool (+0125 Dover).

The southwest-going stream begins –0030 Ullapool (–0450 Dover).

Close to the islands, streams run at up to 3 knots, and heavy tide rips extend right across the channel between Dun and Levenish when wind and tide are opposed.

Constant –0055 Ullapool (–0515 Dover)

Height in metres

MHWS	MHWN	MTL	MLWN	MLWS
3·3	2·5	1·8	1·2	0·4

Dangers and marks

Levenish, over a mile east of Dun at the southeast point of Hirta, is 55 metres high. Rocks which dry 1·5 metres extend a short distance from Levenish, but there are no other hidden dangers.

Directions

Departure for St Kilda might be taken from Berneray (49 miles), Monach Isles (34 miles) or Vaccasay (53 miles), and in clear settled weather an overnight passage could be made, but there are no lights to assist such a passage except the leading lights at St Kilda which have a range of 3 miles.

St Kilda, Village Bay

Norman Smith

Lights

Stornoway CG has pointed out that they are unable to receive traffic from yachts in Village Bay, so that yachts reporting arrival should do so before entering the bay.

Ldg Lts 270° Oc.5s26/38m3M

Anchorage

Anchor in Village Bay at the southeast side of Hirta, the main island of the group, southwest of the pier or northeast of the front leading light. Keep clear of the approach to the slip on the northwest side of the bay, which is used by supply vessels, sometimes at night. There is almost always some swell, and landing at the west side of the pier is tricky. In southerly and easterly winds which are any more than light the anchorage becomes untenable.

As a last resort in heavy weather from south or east shelter might be found in Loch a' Ghlinne (Glen Bay) on the north side of Hirta but depths are too great for anchoring except very close to the shore, and winds are accelerated by the cliffs.

Supplies

Small shop and pub at MOD camp; water, showers at MOD commander's discretion.

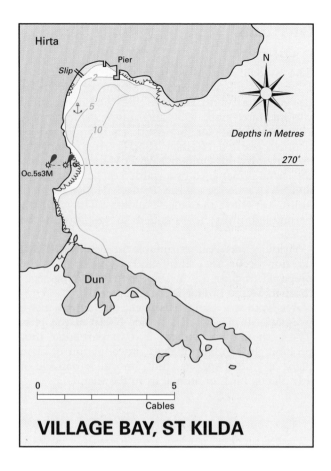

VILLAGE BAY, ST KILDA

St Kilda

The west side of Harris and Lewis

The first 8 miles north of the entrance to Sound of Harris are fairly free from concealed hazards. Further north there are several areas of submerged and drying rocks with few marks by which to avoid them and a visit to the west coast of Harris and Lewis should only be undertaken in clear settled weather.

Chart

2841 (1:50,000) is essential for navigating in this area, although you could manage as far as Taransay with Imray chart *C66*. OS maps *13, 18*. OS Explorer *455, 456, 458*

Tides

The north-going stream, with the east-going stream towards the Sound of Harris begins +0550 Ullapool (+0130 Dover). The south-going stream, with the west-going stream from the Sound of Harris begins –0020 Ullapool (–0440 Dover).

Lights

The following lights give some assistance on this passage:
Haskeir (57°42'N 7°41'·3W) Fl.20s23M
Whale Rock (57°54'·9N 8°00'·7W) E card pillar buoy Q(3)10s
Gasker (57°54'·9N 7°17'·2W) Fl(3)10s38m10M
Flannan Isles (57°54'·9N 8°00'·7W) Fl(2)30s20M
Aird Laimishader, at the east side of the entrance to Loch Roag Fl.6s63m8M

Passage notes – Toe Head to Gallan Head

Dangers and marks

Scarp island lies 11 miles north of Toe Head.

Taransay Glorigs, an extensive area of rocks above water, drying and submerged, lie 3 miles off the mouth of West Loch Tarbert, and Old Rocks lie between Taransay Glorigs and Scarp. For clearing marks see West Loch Tarbert, below.

Barcadale heading for the west of Harris

Looking towards Taransay over NW end of Ensay in the Sound of Harris

Gasker, 30 metres high, lies 4 miles WSW of Scarp. Obe Rocks, drying and submerged, extend up to 6 cables west of Scarp.

Drying, submerged and above-water rocks lie up to 1½ miles north and northwest of Scarp. Old Rocks and Obe Rocks almost always break in the swell. Bomore Rock, 5½ cables offshore, 1½ miles north of Mealasta, nearly dries.

Ard More Mangersta has radio masts and Gallan Head, 4 miles NNE, has a radio mast 177 metres in height. Sgeir Gallan, 3 cables NNW of Gallan Head, dries 3·4 metres.

Directions

From Toe Head steer toward Gasker, and pass midway between Gasker Beg and Scarp. 3 miles past Scarp a course can be steered towards Ard More Mangersta.

From north head for Gasker; a direct course from Ard More Mangersta to Gasker passes ¾ mile west of Bomore Rock (5 miles north of Scarp) and a mile west of rocks northwest of Scarp, so that position checks have to be kept carefully. When Scarp is abeam a course can be steered direct for the passage between Coppay and Toe Head, but the position relative to Old Rocks and Taransay Glorigs still needs to be watched. From Toe Head to Caolas an Scarp, pass east of Taransay Glorigs.

Taransay

57°54'N 6°59'W

Tides

Constant −0053 Ullapool (−0513 Dover)

Height in metres

MHWS	MHWN	MTL	MLWN	MLWS
4·2	3·2	2·3	1·3	0·4

Dangers and marks

Drying rocks lie up to 7 cables south of Taransay; if passing through the Sound of Taransay keep the summit of Coppay in line with Toe Head 244° to pass southeast of Bo Usbig (it is quite easy to confuse Shillay with Coppay). When Aird Nisabost is abeam on the starboard side take a mid-channel course through the sound. In Sound of Taransay Corran Raah and Luskentyre Banks reduce the navigable passage to ½ mile wide. Bo Raah lies 2 cables off Taransay, 4 cables south of Corran Raah, at a depth of 1 metre.

Anchorages

Northside Sands, 57°50'N 7°04'W, is an occasional anchorage at the west side of Borve Bay (Camus nam Borgh) 2 miles east of Toe Head. Drying reefs extend 1½ cables off the west point of the bay. Good holding and shelter in strong southerly winds can be found 1½ cables SSE of Sgeir Leomadal 7 cables west of Northside Sands.

Loch na h-Uidhe, Taransay, 57°53'·5N 7°03'W, on the south side of sandy isthmus joining the two parts of the island. Approaching from Toe Head steer for the south side of Aird Vanish, the west part of the island, to avoid Old Rocks (not to be confused with rocks of the same name south of Scarp) which dry 0·5 metre, 7 cables offshore.

Take care to avoid a detached rock awash about

View A   Mealasta I.   219ft Summit   Liongam I.

219ft summit of Mealasta I. open west of Liongam Island clears Bo Thorcuil to the westward.

View B

Entrance to Loch Tamanavay   Loch Tealasavay

Creagan Gorra Cleite open south of north side of Loch Tealasavay clears Bo Thorcuil to the southward.

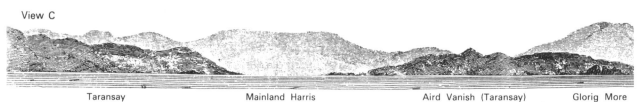

View C

Taransay   Mainland Harris   Aird Vanish (Taransay)   Glorig More

To clear Bo More bring one third of Aird Vanish (Taransay) open to the westward of Glorig More.

Loch na h-Uidhe, Taransay   *Gillian Smith*

two cables offshore, off the end of the reef which extends from Aird Vanish.

Steer towards Ben Raah, the highest point of Taransay until past the middle of the entrance, to clear a rock 1 metre high 2 cables from the west side of the inlet; a reef awash extends northeast from this rock which should be given a wide berth. Langaraid which dries 2·9 metres lies nearly 4 cables off the southwest shore of Taransay and, with Bo Usbig, is in the way when passing between Loch na h-Uidhe and Sound of Taransay.

Traigh Nisabost, 57°52'N 6°58'W, is an occasional anchorage off a sandy bay east of Aird Nisabost at the south side of Traigh Luskentyre on Harris; like any other sandy beach on the west side of the Outer Hebrides it should be treated with great caution because of the swell and even if you can get ashore you may have difficulty getting off again.

Sound of Taransay, 57°54'N 6°59'W. For passage notes see above. Anchor close inshore at the north side of Corran Raah, or in northwest wind, south of the spit, but look out for Bo Raah.

West Loch Tarbert

57°56'N 7°00'W

Tides

The in-going stream begins +0550 Ullapool (+0130 Dover).
The out-going stream begins –0020 Ullapool (–0440 Dover)
Constant –0053 Ullapool (–0513 Dover)

Height in metres

MHWS	MHWN	MTL	MLWN	MLWS
4·2	3·2	2·3	1·3	0·4

Dangers and marks

In the main channel north of Taransay, the Taransay Glorigs, a patch of rocks above and below water lies up to 3 miles from the northeast side of the entrance. Gloruig More (Gloruig Sgoillte), the highest of these is 12 metres high, and the most southerly rock is 1·5 metres high. A submerged rock, Bo Molach, lies 6 cables WSW of Gloruig More.

Old Rocks, which dry up to 2·3 metres, lie up to 3 miles NNW of the Taransay Glorigs. A clearing mark for the most westerly of these, Bo More which dries 0·8 metre, is as follows. Aird Vanish, the west part of Taransay, appears from a distance of several miles to be a separate island, and keeping one-third of the width of Aird Vanish open west of Gloruig More 330° leads clear west of Bo More, see View C on page 126.

Caolas Scarp, from Scarp   *Gillian Smith*

Caolas Scarp from the mainland   *Gillian Smith*

Gasker, 30 metres high, lies 6 miles WNW of Gloruig More with Gasker Beg a mile ESE of it. Drying rocks lie up to 2 cables north of Taransay. Soay Mor and Soay Beag, both 35 metres high, lie ½ mile from the northeast side of Loch Tarbert with Duisker, 2 metres high 9 cables ESE of Soay Mor. Many drying rocks lie between Duisker and Soay Mor and the shore.

Fish cages are moored in Isay Sound, NE of Soay Mor.

Isay, 17 metres high, lies in the middle of the loch 1½ miles ESE of Duisker with a reef also named Duisker ½ mile NNE of it.

In clear visibility the approach to West Loch Tarbert presents no problem.

Anchorages

Loch Leosavay, 57°57'N 7°00'W, is 1 mile northwest of Soay Beag. Glas Sgeir, 8 metres high, stands on a drying reef a cable wide near the northeast side of the entrance of the loch. There is a small shop, post office and telephone at a pink house at the head of the loch.

A rock which just dries lies off the pier in the main loch. Another drying rock lies off the steps built into the sea wall in front of the mansion house on the east side of the loch.

The main loch is reported to have good holding, but the bay in front of the house, on the east side of the loch, is a poor anchorage.

Loch Meavaig, 57°56'N 6°55'W, NNE of the outer Duisker is entered by the southeast side of that rock and east of Bo Harainish which dries 1·1 metres, west of a direct line from Duisker to the entrance. The head of the loch dries off 4 cables, with several large drying rocks spread along the low water line, and it is prone to swell.

Loch Bun Abhainn-eader (Bunaveneadar), 57°56'N 6°52'W, 1 mile northeast of Isay, is identified by a conspicuous chimney. It may be entered either side of the east Duisker, but if passing north of it keep closer to the north shore of the loch as a reef with a depth of 0·1 metre extends up to 2 cables north of Duisker.

Anchor to suit wind direction, clear of fish cages. Shelter is reported to be excellent; the bottom is firm black mud although foul in places. Landing is difficult; best at steps at the steep slip of the old whaling station. There is a shop (licensed) and garage on the southwest side of the loch, uphill by road. It may be more accessible from the fish farm slip on the south side of the loch.

Head of West Loch Tarbert Anchor west of the jetty on the south side; this anchorage is subject to squalls in southerly winds, and swell in northwesterly wind, in which case Bunaveneadar provides good shelter.

Supplies

At Tarbert, ½ mile, see Chapter IV, page 98. Diesel at West Loch Tarbert.

Scarp

58°01'N 7°08'W

Dangers and marks

Taransay Glorigs and *Old Rocks*, south of Scarp, together with a clearing mark for their west side, have been described at West Loch Tarbert, above.

Hushinish Glorigs, above water and drying, lie 6 cables south of Hushinish Point, on Harris south of Scarp. Hushinish Point, in line with the right fall of the summit of Scarp 350°, leads east of Old Rocks and Taransay Glorigs, and close west of Hushinish Glorigs, but this line is not clearly defined.

Caolas an Scarp separates the island from Harris, with a sand bar ¼ mile north of the narrowest part of the passage, on which the charted depth, near the Scarp side of the channel, is 1 metre but there seems to be less water. A northerly swell would make this passage dangerous. Several drying rocks lie between Fladday, north of Caolas an Scarp, and Harris. Anchor either north or south of the sand bar.

Braigh Mor

58°02'N 7°05'W

Braigh Mor is the sound between Lewis and the northeast side of Scarp, leading to several sheltered lochs.

Tides

Tidal streams are slight
Constant –0053 Ullapool (–0513 Dover)
Height in metres

MHWS	MHWN	MTL	MLWN	MLWS
4·2	3·2	2·3	1·3	0·4

Dangers and marks

Obe Rocks, submerged and drying, lie up to 6 cables west of Scarp.

A patch of rocks lies up to 1½ miles north and northwest of Scarp with yet another rock named *Duisker*, 6 metres in height, at the east end.

In the passage between Duisker and Kearstay, an islet north of Scarp, rocks which dry 2·3 metres lie up to 1½ cables from both sides, leaving a clear passage 3 cables wide, but there are no leading marks.

There is a clear passage 1½ miles wide between Duisker and Mealasta, at the north side of the entrance.

Anchorages

An attractive anchorage, sheltered from the open sea, lies between Kearstay and Scarp.

Loch Resort

4 miles long and generally no more than ¼ mile wide. The loch is entered 2 miles east of Scarp.

Greine Sgeir, an islet 6 metres high with reefs drying 1 cable off all sides, lies in mid-channel.

A drying rock lies 2 cables off the south shore, west of Loch Cravadale where there is an occasional anchorage at the head of the bay.

Anchor near the head of the loch, or at Diriscal, 2½ miles from the entrance on the south side with good holding on black smelly mud.

Loch Tealasavay

A mile north of Loch Resort, has only a small area at the south side of the head with moderate depths in which to anchor, but the sea comes straight in so that it is only an occasional anchorage.

Loch Hamnaway

(Tamanavay on the chart) is entered north of Loch Tealasavay.

Bo Thorcuil is a patch of submerged rocks 3 cables from the north shore west of the entrance. Creagan Gorra Cleite, at the head of Loch Tealasavay, showing in the middle of the entrance 079° (View B page 126, and the right-hand summit of Mealasta open west of Liongam 322° (View A page 126) lead south and southwest of Bo Thorcuil.

Anchor close to the head of the loch, or at the east side of the promontory on the south side.

Mealasta

Lies ½ mile from Lewis at the north side of the entrance to Braigh Mor. Caolas an Eilean, between Mealasta and Lewis, provides a tenuous anchorage in settled weather.

Bo Caolas which dries extends 2 cables from the Lewis shore at the north end of the sound. Islands and rocks lie more than a mile offshore for more than a mile north of Mealasta, with a reasonably clear channel inshore.

Bomore Rock 5½ cables offshore, 1½ miles north of Mealasta, nearly dries.

Camas Uig

58°12'N 7°05'W

Provides an occasional anchorage, particularly in a well sheltered pool in 3 metres, behind two small islets in the southeast corner off Carnish. Enter by the southwest side of the more southerly islet.

A guesthouse nearby provides meals. Shop, post office and garage at Timsgarry, about 2½ miles east.

Flannan Islands

58°17'N 7°35'W

A group of rocky islands 17 miles west of Lewis with a lighthouse, occasionally visited by yachts although there is no anchorage. The bottom is bare rock and the large-scale Admiralty chart shows few

Flannan Isles, from south   *Gillian Smith*

soundings.

Of the two landing places the concrete steps of the western one have been washed away. In a legendary incident in 1900 three lighthouse-keepers disappeared, and it is supposed that they were washed off the landing place by an exceptional wave.

Chart
Plan (1:15,000) on chart *2524*.

Loch Roag

58°15'N 6°54'W

A remarkable group of lochs which could occupy a fortnight of exploring with a small boat if it were not for the difficulty of getting there.

Launching places for trailed boats are provided at Miavaig, Valtos and Kirkibost.

Bus from Miavaig and Bernera (Breaclete and Kirkibost) enables crew changes in this area by air or ferry.

Charts
2515 (1:25,000). The two charts *3381*, *3422* (1:12,500) which have been withdrawn may be useful because of their large scale, but make sure they are corrected up to date. OS map *13*. OS Explorer *458*.

Tides
Off the entrance the northeast-going stream begins –0420 Ullapool (+0345 Dover). The southwest-going stream begins +0205 Ullapool (–0215 Dover). The spring rate is knot

The in-going stream begins +0600 Ullapool (+0140 Dover). The out-going stream begins –0010 Ullapool (–0430 Dover); streams reach 1 knot in the narrower channels

Constant –0053 Ullapool (–0513 Dover)

Height in metres

MHWS	MHWN	MTL	MLWN	MLWS
4·2	3·2	2·3	1·3	0·4

Dangers and marks
The entrance is 7 miles wide between Gallan Head,

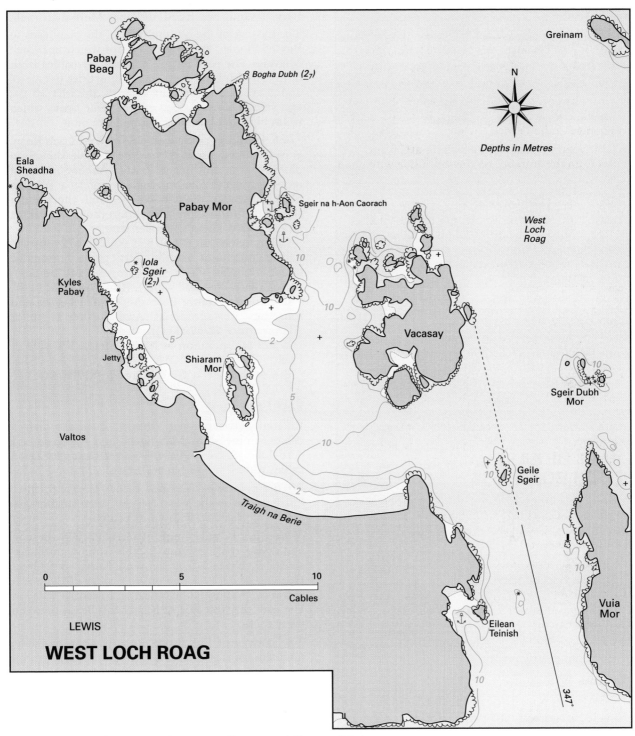

Greinam

Pabay
Beag

Bogha Dubh (2₇)

N

Depths in Metres

Eala
Sheadha

Pabay Mor

Sgeir na h-Aon Caorach

*West
Loch
Roag*

Iola
Sgeir
(2₇)

Kyles
Pabay

Vacasay

Sgeir Dubh
Mor

Jetty

Shiaram
Mor

Valtos

10

Geile
Sgeir

Traigh na Berie

0   5   10

Cables

LEWIS

WEST LOCH ROAG

Eilean
Teinish

Vuia
Mor

347°

on which stands a conspicuous radio mast 170
metres high, and Aird Laimishader, on which stands
a small light beacon, a white hut 5 metres high at
about 60 metres above sea level.

Sgeir Gallan, which dries 3·4 metres, lies ¼ mile
NNW of Gallan Head. Between these points are
scattered many islets, and the two parts of Loch
Roag are separated by Great Bernera.

Old Hill, an islet 92 metres high, shaped like a loaf
of bread, and Mas Sgeir, 21 metres high – each lie
1½ miles northwest and north respectively of Little
Bernera.

Lights

The radio mast on Gallan Head has white aero warning
lights, 275m, with F.R lights on lower masts nearby.
Aird Laimishader Fl.6s63m8M

West Loch Roag

Entered between Pabay Mor on its west side and
Harsgeir, 12 metres high, 1¼ miles ENE of Pabay
Mor. An anchorage which could be reached without
the large-scale chart is on the east side of Pabay
Mor, in the inlet northwest of Sgeir na h-Aon
Chaorach which has a sandy beach at its head.

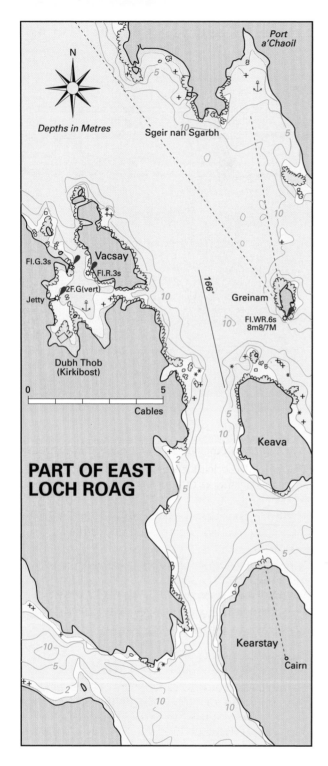

PART OF EAST LOCH ROAG

Berie, a sandy beach SSE of Pabay More if no swell.

The passage at the bottom right of the plan leads to Bay of Floday, at the west end of which lies Loch Miavaig. The rock in mid channel 1½ cables ENE of Eilean Teinish, Bogha na Muilne, dries 0·9 metre and is avoided by keeping Liacam, the islet off the east side of Vacsay, open east of Geile Sgeir, which is 4m high and has an unpainted can on it.

Loch Miavaig, at the west side of West Loch Roag, is well sheltered and the overhead cable shown on older charts no longer exists. Anchor clear of moorings which are in shallow water; a suitable place is between the jetty on the south shore and a slip on the north shore. Shop, post office and garage at Timsgarry, about 2½ miles west.

Calum Morrison (☎ 01851 672285/672444) will deliver purchases to the jetty given reasonable notice. Supplies Calor Gas (propane and butane), petrol, diesel (red and white). Also Post Office.

Community centre near shop with tearoom and museum. Restaurant at Aird further 2 miles (Bonaventure ☎ 672474).

Water and pontoon at Miavaig jetty (SW side of Loch).

Bus to Stornoway from Miavaig and Bernera.

East Loch Roag

Entered between Sgeir Dhearg, 2 metres high 3 cables southeast of Mas Sgeir, and Craigeam off Aird Laimishader. There is also a clear passage 3 cables wide south of Sgeir Dhearg.

Loch Carloway, described below, is easy to enter but exposed to the west. Several other anchorages can be approached without difficulty.

Keava lies ¼ mile south of Greinam light beacon and drying rocks lie up to a cable from its northeast shore. In Kyles Keava between Keava and Great Bernera drying rocks lie on both sides of the north entrance. A conspicuous cairn on Eilean Kearstay in line with the west side of Keava 166° leads between these rocks.

The fairway of East Loch Roag is clean as far as Greinam, an islet 1 cable across about 5 miles within the loch in the middle of the fairway, with a white light beacon 5 metres high at its south end. Rocks over which the depth is less than 2 metres lie up to 2 cables from either shore, but the clear passage is still 4 cables wide.

Kearstay lies ¼ mile south of Keava, with a passage ½ cable wide on its east side and a passage 1 cable wide on its west side. In the east passage a submerged rock lies a cable north of a promontory on the east side of the channel, and a drying rock lies ¼ cable northwest of the same promontory. The west passage has rocks awash and drying up to ¼ cable from its west side.

Lights
Aird Laimishader Fl.6s63m8M

Bogha Bhealt, which dries 2·4 metres, and is about ½ cable across, lies a cable southeast of Sgeir na h-Aon Chaorach and an alternative anchorage lies southwest of this rock, although it may be troubled by swell when the rock covers.

A submerged rock lies in the middle of the south end of the sound on the east side of Pabay Mor, and a rock which dries 2·7 metres lies in the middle of Kyles Pabay. Many other anchorages may be found with chart *2515*.

Water and showers at caravan site at Traigh na

Carloway pier

Greinam Fl.WR.6s8m8/7M
Breaclete Pier (east of Keava) 2F.R(vert)10/7m4M

Lights

Lights in Loch Carloway and at Dubh Thob are described below.

Loch Carloway

Waypoint 58°16'·5N 6°49'W

On the east side of the entrance of East Loch Roag ½ mile south of Aird Laimishader light beacon.

Tin Rocks, in the middle of the loch, are marked on their north side by a green conical buoy.

Dunan Pier stands at the north side of the head of the loch and a shoal patch with a depth of 1 metre lies in the middle of the loch 1½ cables WSW of the

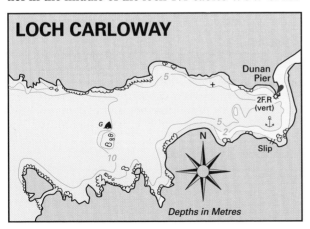

pier. Good holding south of the pier in black mud.

The arm of the loch northeast of the pier is shoal, but provides shelter at neaps or for shallow-draught boats.

A slip in the southeast corner of the loch is convenient for landing to visit the broch of Dun Carloway.

A light 2F.R(vert) stands at the head of Dunan Pier.

Supplies and services

Shop, post office; water at the pier. Diesel. Hotel 2M south of Carloway. 1-ton crane.

Anchorages in East Loch Roag

Bernera Harbour, 58°15'·5N 6°52'W, (Kyles of Little Bernera) is on the west side of East Loch Roag about 2 miles south of Mas Sgeir. The passage at the west end of Bernera Harbour (Camas Cumhany) has a least depth (at its east end) of 0·6 metre.

Cruitir, 3 metres high on an extensive reef, lies nearly 4 cables east of Little Bernera with drying rocks inshore of it.

Rocks which dry 0·7 metre on the south side of the inlet within the entrance extend to mid-channel.

Further in, Sgeir a' Chaolais which dries 1·9 metres is marked on its south side by a beacon with a black-and-white cage topmark, fish cages are moored east and west of Sgeir a'Chaolais and a submerged rock lies ½ cable from the south shore 1 cable west of Sgeir a' Chaolais.

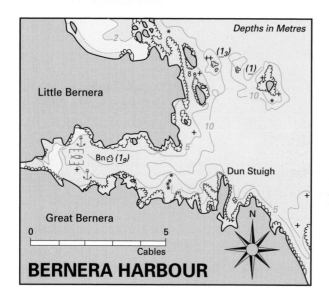

BERNERA HARBOUR

Kirkibost (Dubh Thob) Loch Roag, looking towards the northern entrance

Keep to the north of mid-channel on entering, pass south of Sgeir a' Chaolais and anchor off the ruin on the northwest side of the inlet.

Water at fish farm shed at slip on south shore. Breaclete for stores (see below) 2 miles. Bostadh Beach Iron Age Village with reconstructed dwelling ½ mile west.

Loch Risay, 57°13'·9N 6°49'·2W. The pool at the head of the loch is recommended for a remote anchorage. A restored 'norse mill' stands at the outlet from two freshwater lochs on the west shore, and a path from there leads to Breaclete where facilities include a phone, post office and shop, as well as a small museum.

Dubh Thob 58°13'N 6°48'W (also known as Kirkibost) is an enclosed basin between Great Bernera and Vacasay Island, which lies ½ mile northwest of Greinam.

A narrow and shallow entrance from the east lies south of Vacasay, and another with rocks marked by light beacons, from the north.

In the north entrance a metal column 2 metres high marks a drying rock on the east side of the passage, and another stands on the shore on the west side, but drying reefs extend beyond this mark, and the clear channel is about a third of a cable wide.

A jetty stands on the west side of the basin and a reef extends from the south shore to within ½ cable east of the jetty.

Lights

Fl.R.3s2m2M light on the drying rock west of Vacasay
Fl.G.3s2m2M light on shore on the west side of the channel
Kirkibost jetty 2F.G(vert)

Supplies and services

Water and diesel at pier, public toilets, telephone.

Stores (licensed), post office, community centre with showers and local museum at Breaclete, 3 miles. Alternatively anchor at Loch Risay or Loch Beag Breaclete.

Port a' Chaoil, 58°14'N 6°46'·5W, on the east shore of East Loch Roag, mile north of Greinam, is sheltered from seaward.

Sgeir nan Sgarbh which dries 1·9 metres lies a third of a cable south of the west point of the bay, and a rock which dries 1·3 metres lies about ½ cable off the middle of the head of the bay, with a submerged rock further south.

Rocks submerged and drying lie on a line between the east side of the bay and Greinam.

Breasclete, 58°13'N 6°45'W, east of Keava. Anchor south of old jetty which is east of the conspicuous factory and pier at Rubha Arspaig. Shop 200 metres left at crossroads. Water at the pier.

Callanish, 58°11'·5N 6°45'W; the best place from which to visit the standing stones is the anchorage east of Bratanish Islands which lies about ¼ mile east of the south end of Kearstay.

Power cables with headroom of 5·7 metres cross the passage ¼ mile southeast of the islands.

A submerged rock lies one-third of a cable south of Bratanish Mor, the west island, and another lies one-third of a cable off the east shore of the inlet.

Supplies

Restaurant at Garrynahine, 1M SW of Callanish.

Passage notes – Gallan Head to Butt of Lewis and Tiumpan Head

Tiumpan Head is at the end of the Eye Peninsula, east of Stornoway on the east side of Lewis. To avoid confusion, note that a point about 1½ miles north of Aird Laimishader is also named Tiumpan.

Charts

2720 1:200 000. OS Explorer *460* (+*459*). OS Landranger *8*

Tides at the Butt of Lewis

The northeast, east and south-going stream begins –0435 Ullapool (+0335 Dover)

The north, west and southwest-going stream begins +0150 Ullapool (–0230 Dover)

The spring rate in each direction is 4 to 5 knots close to the point, with eddies on the downstream side of the point

About a mile offshore the streams run at 3 knots; the point should be given a berth of at least 5 miles, which must be allowed for in calculating the length of the passage, unless the wind is both fair in direction and moderate in strength, and the tide is going in the same direction.

Tidal streams on the northwest side of Lewis turn 15 minutes later and run at 1½ knots at springs. Tidal streams on the east side of Lewis turn about an hour earlier and the maximum spring rate is 2 knots.

The distance from Gallan Head to the Butt of Lewis is about 30 miles, 17 from the Butt of Lewis to Tiumpan Head, and a further 13 to Stornoway. The Butt of Lewis is completely exposed to weather from southwest through north to southeast and there is no shelter between Loch Roag and Stornoway except the new fishing harbour at Brevig in Broad Bay (but see page 115), north of Eye Peninsula, the head of which gives some shelter from southwest.

Dangers and marks

Aird Laimishader lies 7 miles northeast of Gallan Head, and the islets in the mouth of Loch Roag between them are conspicuous.

Hen Shoal, a mile offshore, 7 miles southwest of the Butt of Lewis, at a depth of 9 metres, may cause some disturbance at the surface.

Port of Ness, on the east side of Lewis 2 miles southeast of the lighthouse, provides some shelter from the west in a sandy bay with moderate depths. A drying boat harbour stands on the north side of the bay.

Tolsta Head is prominent with a vertical cliff 66 metres high at its end.

Braga Rock which dries 3·4 metres lies 2 cables offshore 3½ miles southeast of the lighthouse. Tolsta Head open of Cellar Head 180° leads east of the rock.

Tiumpan Head is marked by a white lighthouse tower 21 metres in height.

Lights

Aird Laimishader Fl.6s63m8M
Flannan Islands Fl(2)30s101m20M

Butt of Lewis Fl.5s52m25M
Tiumpan Head Fl(2)15s55m25M

By night these lights are sufficient for a coastal passage in good visibility.

For Stornoway see Chapter V.

Appendix

I. CHARTS AND OTHER PUBLICATIONS

The Imray charts *C65*, *C66* and *C67* at a scale of around 1:150,000 cover the waters referred to in this volume. They are available at most chandlers and from the Clyde Cruising Club, usually folded, but for any boat which has a large enough chart table it is better to order a flat copy and, better still, one laminated in plastic.

Admiralty chart *2635* is a general chart for the whole west coast of Scotland at a scale of 1:500,000.

The following Admiralty charts relate to the waters covered by this volume. Some of these are essential, and the more you have, the less your pilotage will be fraught with anxiety. The relevant Ordnance Survey maps are also listed.

Chart	Title – areas in Chapters I & II	Scale
1796	Barra Head to Ardnamurchan	1:100,000
1795	The Little Minch	1:100,000
2769	Barra Head to Greian Head	1:30,000
2770	Sound of Barra and Loch Boisdale	1:30,000
2825	Lochs on the east coast of Uist	various
2904	Usinish to Eigneig Mor	1:25,000
OS 31	Barra and surrounding islands	1:50,000
OS 22	Benbecula	1:50,000

Chart	Title – areas in Chapter III	Scale
1795	The Little Minch	1:100,000
2825	Lochs on the east coast of Uist	various
2642	Sound of Harris	1:20,000
2841	Sound of Harris to Ard More Mangersta	1:50,000
OS 18	Sound of Harris	1:50,000

Chart	Title – areas in Chapter IV	Scale
1795	The Little Minch	1:100,000
2905	East Loch Tarbert	1:10,000
OS 14	Tarbert and Loch Seaforth	1:50,000

Chart	Title – areas in Chapter V	Scale
1785	North Minch, Northern Part	1:100,000
1794	North Minch, Southern Part	1:100,000
2529	Approaches to Stornoway	1:25,000
OS 8	Stornoway and North Lewis	1:50,000
OS 14	Tarbert and Loch Seaforth	1:50,000

Chart	Title – areas in Chapter VI	Scale
2722	Skerryvore to St Kilda	1:200,000
2721	St Kilda to the Butt of Lewis	1:200,000
2841	Sound of Harris to Ard More Mangersta	1:50,000
2515	Ard More Mangersta to Tiumpan including Loch Roag	various
2524	Islands off the NW Coast of Scotland	various
OS 31	Barra and surrounding islands	1:50,000
OS 22	Benbecula	1:50,000
OS 18	Sound of Harris	1:50,000
OS 13	West Lewis and North Harris	1:50,000

Current charts show less detail ashore than older charts, and Ordnance Survey maps at a scale of 1:50,000 help to fill in the picture.

OS Explorer maps at 1:25,000 may be extremely useful where there is no Admiralty chart at a sufficiently large scale. An index sheet of all OS maps is available from larger bookshops and from Ordnance Survey, Romsey Road, Southampton SO16 4GU ☎ 08456 050505, as well as on the Internet at www.ordnancesurvey.co.uk

There are Admiralty chart agents throughout Britain, and in most other countries. Chart agents are:

Duncan McIver, Stornoway, ☎ 01851 702012
Kelvin Hughes, Glasgow ☎ 0141 429 6462
Imray, Laurie, Norie & Wilson Ltd are Admiralty chart agents and will supply charts by post; Wych House, The Broadway, St Ives, Cambridgeshire PE27 5BT ☎ 01480 462114 *Fax* 01480 496109 email ilmw@imray.com www.imray.com

Some charts which have long been discontinued provide much more detail, at a larger scale, than any now published for the same area. All older charts, particularly the fine Victorian engravings, show more detail inshore and on land than the current publications, although they may be less accurate. Old charts should only be used to supplement current ones, not as a substitute for them.

The following obsolete charts in particular (all published before 1934) may be found useful:
1351 Loch Uskavagh
2805 Monach Isles and approaches
3168 Benbecula, etc., showing more detail than current chart, but current chart must also be used as some submerged rocks have been discovered more recently.

Photocopies of old charts – of editions not less than 50 years old, for copyright reasons – may be obtained from the National Library of Scotland Map Room Annexe, 33 Salisbury Place, Edinburgh 9 ☎ 031 226 4531

The Clyde Cruising Club Sailing Directions and Anchorages are available from the CCC at Suite 408, The Pentagon Centre, Washington St, Glasgow G3 8AZ ☎ 0141 221 2774 *Fax* 0141 221 2775.

The Admiralty West Coast of Scotland Pilot (NP 66) is now published every three years or so without regular Supplements, but any important corrections are published in Weekly Notices to Mariners. The most recent edition was published in 2001.

Admiralty Notices to Mariners, both weekly and quarterly Small Craft Editions are available on the Internet at www.nms.ukho.gov.uk/

The Admiralty Tidal Stream Atlas for the North Coast of Ireland and West Coast of Scotland (NP 218) is very useful.

Tide tables are essential, preferably for Ullapool giving heights of each high and low water.

General books

The Scottish Islands, by Hamish Haswell Smith, is an extremely useful general guide (Canongate, 1996)
Exploring Scotland's Heritage - The Highlands, Joanna Close-Brooks (HMSO, 1986)

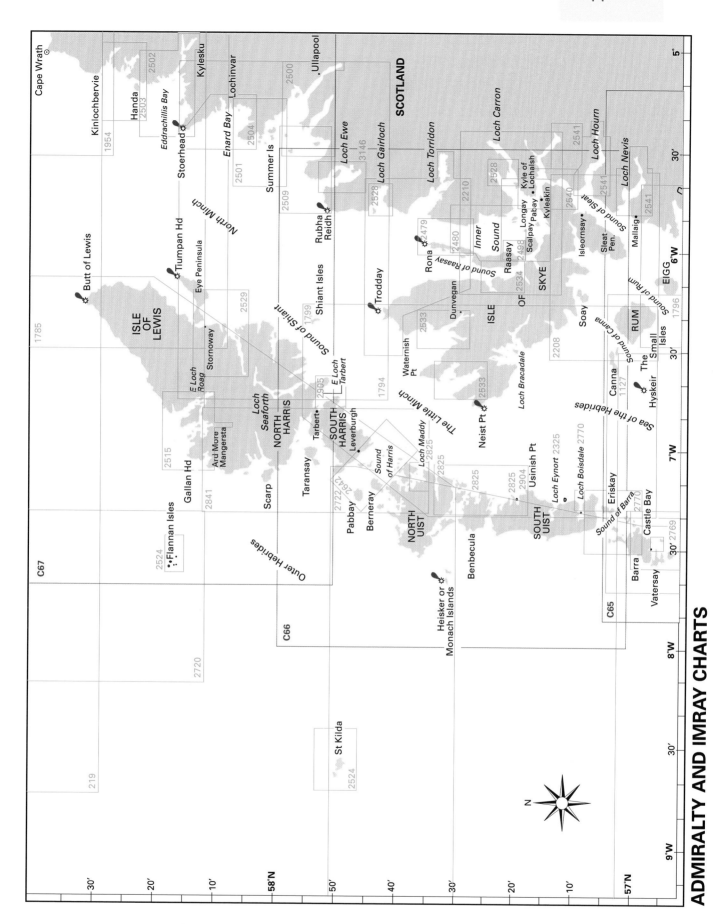

ADMIRALTY AND IMRAY CHARTS

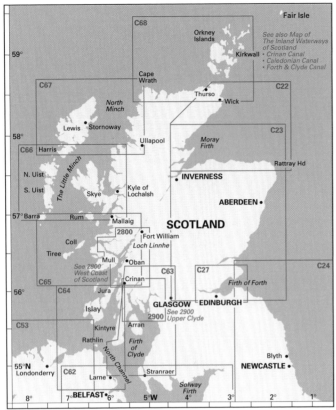

Imray charts

C65 Crinan to Mallaig and Barra
Plans Sound of Luing, Lynn of Lorn,
Tobermory, Castle Bay, Mallaig,
Entrance to Caledonian Canal, Oban 1:150,000

**C66 Mallaig to Rudha Reidh and
Outer Hebrides**
Plans St Kilda, East Loch Tarbert,
Loch Maddy, Loch Carnan,
Loch Boisdale, Dunvegan, Portree,
Loch Gairloch, Kyleakin, Uig 1:150,000

C67 North Minch and Isle of Lewis
Plans Loch Inver, Stornoway
Ullapool, Loch Inchard
(Kinlochbervie), Loch Carloway 1:146,000

The Islands of Scotland including Skye (Scottish Mountaineering Trust, 1989 for climbers and hillwalkers)

II. SLIPS SUITABLE FOR LAUNCHING AND RECOVERING TRAILED BOATS

Although one is likely to launch a trailed boat either near a ferry terminal or near a chosen cruising ground, one might need to recover the boat elsewhere, owing to stress of weather or otherwise. Slips are known to exist at the following locations, although some may be privately owned, or may be obstructed, and some are not surfaced and only suitable for a four wheel drive vehicle:

(WIIC indicates a slip owned by Western Isles Islands Council; there may be a charge for its use)

Vatersay causeway (56°56'N 07°34'W) WIIC
Castlebay (56°56'N 07°31'W) MacBraynes; behind link-span
Eoligarry, north end of Barra (57°01'N 07°26'W) WIIC
Ardveenish (57°00'N 07°25'W) WIIC
Orosay (57°07'N 07°25'W) WIIC
Lochboisdale fishery pier (57°08'N 07°19'W) WIIC
Loch Skipport fish farm (57°20'N 07°16'W) possibly private
Peter's Port (57°23'N 07°15'W) WIIC
Kallin (57°24'N 07°15'W) WIIC
Locheport (57°33'N 07°18'W) not concrete
Lochmaddy (57°36'N 07°09'W) not concrete WIIC. Another, concrete, owned by Mr A Morrison, Harbour View
Cheesebay (57°39'N 07°06'W) WIIC
Newton ferry (57°41'N 07°13'W) WIIC
Leverburgh (57°46'N 07°01'W)
Ceann Dibig, East Loch Tarbert (57°53'N 07°49'W) WIIC
Kyles Scalpay ferry (57°53'N 07°41'W) WIIC
East Tarbert fishery pier/slip (57°54'N 07°49'W) WIIC
Stornoway (58°12'N 06°23'W)
Brevig (57°14'N 06°20'W) WIIC
Kyles Bayhead (57°35'N 07°26'W) sand
Griminish (57°39'N 07°26'W) WIIC not concrete
Port of Ness (58°30'N 06°15'W) WIIC
Kirkibost, Loch Roag (58°13'N 06°48'W) WIIC
Hushinish (Harris) (58°00'N 07°06'W) WIIC

III. QUICK REFERENCE TABLE OF PROVISIONS, SERVICES AND SUPPLIES

Columns

1	Water	A	Alongside, by hose
		T	Tap on jetty or quay
		N	Nearby tap
2	Shop	S	Several, or supermarket
		L	Local, well stocked village store
		B	Basic
3	Diesel	A	Alongside, by hose
		M	Marine diesel, near
		G	Garage
4	Petrol	P	(usually needs to be carried some distance)
5	Calor Gas	C	
6	Repairs	H	Hull
		M	Marine engine
		E	Electronics (engineer may need to come from a distance)
7	Chandlery	Y	Yacht
		F	Fishermen's chandlery
		I	Ironmonger, hardware store, which may be better than nothing
8	Visitors'	V	(including those provided by hotel for customers)
	moorings	P	Pontoon
9	Catering	R	Restaurant
		B	Bar
		S	Showers
10	Bank	£	
11	Rubbish	D	
	disposal		
12	Crane		Capacity in tons

Page	Place, grouped in sequence of chapters	1	2	3	4	5	6	7	8	9	10	11	12
13	Vatersay	.	.	A	.	.	.	.	.	.	.	.	.
13	Castlebay	A	S	G	P		.	FI	V	RBS	£	D	
18	Northbay	A	.	A	.	C	.	.	V	RB	.	.	1
26	Eriskay	T	L1½	.	.	C1½	.	I1½	V	RB1½	£	.	
31	Loch Boisdale	A	S3	G	P	.	.	I	.	RB	.	D	.
47	Kallin	T	.	A	.	.	H	F	V	.	.	D	1
52	Loch Eport	.	L1	.									
57	Lochmaddy	A	L	G	.	C	.	.	V	RBS	£	D	.
61	Lochportain	.	B	.	.	.	.	.	.	.	.	.	.
68	Berneray	A	L	A	.	C	.	.	V	.	.	D	1
76	Leverburgh	T	L	A	P	C	.	.	.	.	.	.	.
81	Finsbay	.	B	.	.	.	.	.	.	.	.	.	.
85	Stockinish	.	.	A	.	.	.	.	.	.	.	.	.
91	Scalpay	T	S	A	P	.	.	.	.	.	.	D	.
95	Tarbert	T	S	C	P	C	.	.	V	RBS	£	D	.
113	Stornoway	A	S	A	P	C	HME	F	P	RBS	£	D	.
115	Brevig	A	.	.	.	.	.	.	.	.	.	.	.
	West Loch Tarbert see Tarbert, above, distance about 1M)	.	.	A									
129	Loch Bunaveneadar	.	L	G	P	.	.	.	.	.	.	.	.
129	Loch Leosavay	.	B	.	.	.	.	.	.	.	.	.	.
132	Miavaig	A	2½	A	.	.	.	.	.	.	.	.	.
134	Kirkibost	A	.	A	.	.	.	.	.	.	.	D	1
134	Breasclete	T	L	.	.	.	.	.	.	.	.	.	.
132	Carloway	T	L	.	.	.	.	.	.	2	.	.	1

Note

Figures following reference letter indicate the distance in miles from the landing place.

IV. GLOSSARY OF GAELIC WORDS WHICH COMMONLY APPEAR IN PLACE NAMES

Many varieties of spelling are found, so it is as well to search for possible alternatives; variations of the same word are listed together but usually at least have the same initial letter. Many words beginning with a consonant take an 'h' after the initial letter in certain cases; notably nouns of the feminine gender and their adjectives, and the genitive cases of many nouns, so that most of the words below could have an 'h' as the second letter.

There is no possibility of guiding the reader on pronunciation except to say that consonants followed by an 'h' are often not pronounced, and that 'mh' and 'bh' at the beginning of a word are pronounced as (and of course in anglicised versions often spelt with) a 'v'. *Mhor* is pronounced – approximately – *vore*; *claidheamh* is something like *clayeh*, and *bogha* is *bo'a*.

Some names, particularly those of islands ending in 'a' or 'ay', are of Norse origin. Anyone at all familiar with French and Latin will see correspondences there, for example Caisteil – also Eaglais and Teampuill.

Many words are compounds made up of several often quite common parts, frequently linked by *na/nam/nan*. The following are the most usual forms of words which commonly occur in Gaelic place names. They often set out to describe the physical features and so give some clues to identification. Some of them occur almost everywhere; most lochs have a Sgeir Mhor and an Eilean Dubh, or vice versa.

Gaelic	*English*
a, an, an t, -a'	the
abhainn (avon)	river
acarsaid	harbour (acair = anchor)
achadh (ach, auch)	field
allt	stream, burn
aird (ard)	promontory
aros	house
ba	cattle
bairneach	limpet
bagh ('bay')	bay
ban	white, pale; as a prefix = female (ban-righ = queen)
bealach	narrow path, pass
beag, beaga (beg)	small
beinn (ben)	mountain
beul (bel)	mouth of (belnahua = mouth of the cave)
bodach	old man
bogha (bo')	a detached rock, usually one which uncovers
breac	speckled (as noun: trout)
buachaille	shepherd
buidhe (buie)	yellow (also: pleasing)
bun	mouth of a river
cailleach	old woman
caisteil	castle
camas	wide bay
caol, caolas, (a' chaolais)	narrow passage (kyle)
caorach	sheep
ceall, cille (keills, kells, kil)	monastic cell, church
ceann (kin...)	head
clachan	usually a group of houses (clach = stone)
claidheamh	sword (hence 'claymore' = great sword)

cnoc (knock)	rounded hill
coire (corrie)	cauldron, hollow among hills, whirlpool
craobh	tree
creag	cliff, rock (crag)
darroch	oak tree
dearg ('jerrig')	red
deas	south
dobhran	otter
donn	brown (dun)
druim	ridge
dubh (dhu)	black, dark, (disastrous)
dun, duin	fortified place, usually prehistoric
each	horse
ear	east
eilean (or eileach)	island
fada	long
fir, fear	man
fraoch, fraoich	heather
garbh	rough
geal	white
gille	boy
glas	grey (sometimes green)
gobhar (gour)	goat (gabhar = she-goat)
gorm	blue
gamhna	stirk, year-old calf
iar	west (easily confused with Ear)
iolair	eagle
keills, kells	church
kin... (ceann)	head of
liath	grey
mara	sea
meadhonach	middle-sized
meall	lump, knob
mor (more, mhor, vore)	large, great (often only relative)
muc, muck	pig (often a sea-pig = porpoise or a whale)
na, na h-, nam, nan of (the)	
naomh (nave, neave)	holy, saint
...nish (ness)	point of land
poll, puill	pool
righ ('ree')	king
ron, roin	seal
ruadh, rudha	red, reddish
rubha (rhu)	point of land, promontory
sailean	creek
sgeir, sgeirean (skerry)	rock, above water or covering
sron	nose (as a headland)
sruth	stream, currenttigh house
tober	well
traigh	beach
tuath (or tuadh)	north
uamh	cave

Index